IN YOUR BEST INTEREST

Author's Note

This book contains numerous numbers, tables, charts, graphs, and calculations. While the author has made every effort to provide accurate information at the time of publishing, neither the publisher nor the author assumes any responsibility for errors or for changes that occur after publishing.

IN YOUR BEST INTEREST

The Ultimate Guide to the Canadian Bond Market

W.H. "HANK" CUNNINGHAM

THE DUNDURN GROUP
TORONTO

Copy-Editor: Andrea Waters
Design: Andrew Roberts
Printer: Webcom

Library and Archives Canada Cataloguing in Publication

Cunningham, W. H.
In your best interest : the ultimate guide to the Canadian bond market / W.H. "Hank" Cunningham.

ISBN-10: 1-55002-578-3
ISBN-13: 978-1-55002-578-1

1. Bond market--Canada. 2. Fixed-income securities--Canada.

HG5154.C85 2006 332.63'23'0971 C2005-906316-5

1 2 3 4 5 10 09 08 07 06

Conseil des Arts du Canada Canada Council for the Arts Canada

ONTARIO ARTS COUNCIL
CONSEIL DES ARTS DE L'ONTARIO

We acknowledge the support of the Canada Council for the Arts and the Ontario Arts Council for our publishing program. We also acknowledge the financial support of the Government of Canada through the Book Publishing Industry Development Program and The Association for the Export of Canadian Books, and the Government of Ontario through the Ontario Book Publishers Tax Credit program, and the Ontario Media Development Corporation.

Printed and bound in Canada.
Printed on recycled paper.

www.dundurn.com

Dundurn Press
3 Church Street, Suite 500
Toronto, Ontario, Canada
M5E 1M2

Gazelle Book Services Limited
White Cross Mills
Hightown, Lancaster, England
LA1 4X5

Dundurn Press
2250 Military Road
Tonawanda NY
U.S.A. 14150

IN YOUR BEST INTEREST

To Caroline and Valerie

Table of Contents

ACKNOWLEDGMENTS

I would like to thank three people who helped make this book a reality: Stuart Henry, the Chief Financial Officer of First Marathon Securities, for believing in me and for supporting me during my twelve years there; Lyman MacInnis, who mentored me, kept me on track, encouraged me to begin (and finish!) this book, and introduced me to my editor; and Alan MacInnis, said editor, who cajoled, needled, and hounded me to finish the book, and with whom my only points of contention were the use of semicolons and long sentences.

INTRODUCTION

"Lift the 29s for 10 at .40."

"Kevin, show the MLI a fifteen-cent bid for the new Saskies."

"Lucy, show the HOOP $100 m. of the thirty-year Ontario resids at +50 and let me know."

"Nat, TAL wants to sell 10s and buy 30s at +50, 100 up."

"Robby, watch your bids. I hear there is a big Ontario issue coming."

"What the ##@@! happened? The bottom fell out of this market."

What are these people talking about? Why is it relevant? This is typical language heard in institutional bond trading departments. The first phrase has to do with a Canada trader instructing an interdealer broker to buy $10 million Government of Canada 5.75 percent June 1, 2029, at a price of $121.40, from an anonymous seller. The other phrases involve bond traders telling institutional salespeople to suggest certain transactions to their customers, salespeople telling their traders what their institutional customers would like to do, and a manager telling the traders and salespeople that a big new issue of Ontario bonds is about to hit the market. This language is analogous to sports terminology. It is all about what happens "between the white lines" (a phrase that might be associated with baseball or football) — there is a whole separate code of conduct and language that is familiar to the participants but not to the spectators. It is the shorthand of the business, likely unintelligible to you.

In the major financial centres all over the world, thousands of traders, salespeople, economists, central bankers, portfolio managers, hedge fund managers, company treasurers, and finance ministers, to name but a few, are constantly analyzing inflation, money supply growth, economic growth, budget deficits and surpluses, credit ratings, supply and demand, and a host of other economic factors. The net result is that this collection of people and organizations contributes to establishing the price of the commodity known as money; this is more commonly known as the level of interest rates. Interest rates, in turn, affect just about every major financial decision in life, from whether to buy a house (through analyzing mortgage rates) to how much income you will receive when you retire. You should learn about all aspects of the fixed-income markets, since that is where interest rates are set and where you can earn more income. The financial services industry has failed in educating individual investors, instead pushing products at investors without thinking very much about the suitability of those products. What is in *it's* self-interest is seldom in *your* best interest.

The purpose of this book is to equip you with the knowledge and tools needed to maximize your returns while protecting your principal. In these days of low interest rates, investors bemoan the good old days when bonds yielded 11 percent. They forget that inflation was 8.5 percent back then. Now, with ten-year government bonds at 4 percent and inflation at 1.5 percent, real interest rates — bond yields minus inflation — are actually the same: 2.5 percent! Even so, these lower nominal yields have made investors focus more on their income needs. This is especially true for the baby boomers who have passed their peak spending days, are setting their sights on their retirement years, and are planning to have adequate savings to retire with. A high proportion of these individuals have paid off their mortgages, often their children have graduated and have careers of their own, and perhaps they have sold the family residence and moved to a smaller dwelling or to the country, taking out some cash in the process. This point takes on special relevance after the post-bubble fallout. (This dramatic term refers to how investors have reacted to the stunning fall in value of hundreds of growth stocks whose market value melted to a small fraction of what it had been at the peak of the market bubble.) Many investors were counting on retiring on the future value of these growth icons.

This is not an "I told you so" book. The principles I espouse here are applicable at any stage of an economic or market cycle. Investors have learned that they cannot rely solely on equity markets for their retirement needs. The principles of preservation of capital and returns on that capital have returned to the forefront of investing, and as retirement draws nearer, investors are starting to realize that fixed-income investments should constitute a healthy percentage of their portfolios. The principles explained in this book may be applied at any time and in any investment cycle, by investors of any age. I could have written this in the middle of the bubble and it would have carried the same message: individual investors, by adopting and employing simple principles, can produce solid returns via investing in high-quality individual fixed-income securities. What this equity-market volatility has underscored is the need for investors to invest their savings in the different categories of investments appropriate to their ages and circumstances. This mixture of investments is more commonly labelled the "asset mix." The most common categories in which to invest your money are bank deposits (cash), treasury bills, common equities (stocks), real estate, GICs, and bonds. Within each category, you can deploy your money in different ways. Within common equities, for example, you could invest in solid, dividend-paying banks and utilities or in aggressive, high-growth, high-risk technology stocks. In bonds, you could buy Canada Savings Bonds, corporate bonds, or high-yield or "junk" bonds.

Generally, the younger you are, the more you will invest in equities and real estate. As you age and enter your peak savings years, with an empty nest and no mortgage, your thoughts begin to move towards building an adequate retirement pot to provide you with enough income. This is the time when your asset mix should become more skewed to individual fixed-income securities whose income stream and future value are known, away from the more volatile and unpredictable equity securities. You will still have some equities, but they will more than likely be conservative, dividend-paying ones. This is not a time for fixed-income mutual funds, as their future value and income level are uncertain, but more on this later.

Accentuating the importance of this asset mix is demography. The baby boom is in or entering its peak earning years. As people age and their assets grow, they want more personal attention and individualized solutions for their investment needs. This partly explains why mutual funds are falling from favour and why there has been a marked growth in individually managed portfolios, investment counsellors, and self-directed individual portfolios. Simply put, mutual funds cannot differentiate one investor from another and thus cannot offer any specific solutions. Recent scandals have further increased investors' distrust.

One analogy from a book about demographics and the financial markets explains this.[1] Mutual funds of today are akin to the cheap beer of university days. While we may drink less today, we want the beer to be high quality, or perhaps we now prefer a fine wine. This analogy is particularly appropriate for the fixed-income markets, where bond mutual funds are just not appropriate for retirement planning in that returns, income, and future values are all uncertain.

I will show you how to achieve solid, certain returns by focusing on a specific strategy and on specific securities. The laddering strategy involves investing monies in fixed-income investments of different but evenly spaced maturities. This strategy has stood the test of time, and it will continue to do so. It has outperformed, and will continue to outperform, the majority of bond mutual funds whose

---

[1]David Cork. *The Pig and the Python: How to Prosper From the Aging Baby Boom*. Toronto: Stoddart Books, 1996.

managers charge too much for merely average performance. The laddered approach takes the guesswork out of the direction of interest rates and allows investors to own individual fixed-income securities with a defined income stream and a known future value. In addition, there are very valuable, retail-investor-friendly investment products called zero coupon bonds that are excellent retirement planning tools; they provide investors with the precise future nominal value of their money. These bonds, when combined with the laddered approach, are ideal for RRSPs. For taxable income needs, I again recommend the laddered approach, but using interest-bearing provincial and corporate bonds for their higher yield. Mutual bond funds, you may have noticed, are not part of this strategy.

By demystifying the fixed-income market and educating you in all of its aspects, I will show you how to meet your income and retirement needs and make the retail fixed-income market less expensive, less formidable, more accessible, and more efficient. In other words, I want to make you wealthier. That could mean increasing your net worth and your income, making your retirement portfolio bigger, or allowing you to retire sooner.

The prime reason I am in this business is to make my clients better off by offering them excellent service and advice. A high percentage of investment advisors (IAs), however, merely sell products and do not focus on their clients' needs. Thus, it is in your best interest to not only learn about the fixed-income markets and how they work but also select an IA who can help you satisfy your needs. After reading this book, you will be able to buy and sell individual bonds, and you will know how to choose the appropriate ones, how to build your own portfolio, and where you can find a good IA.

The following sections are included in the book: what the bond market is, how it functions, the various products, how to use this market profitably, winning strategies, how to find and choose an IA, the mathematics of bonds, the concept of duration, bonds for the speculator, retirement planning (RRSPs and RRIFs), reinvestment risk, and finally bond mutual funds and GICs versus individual fixed-income products. There are separate chapters for zero coupon bonds and for the laddered approach, as they represent the cornerstones of your retirement needs. As an added bonus, you will know which way bond prices go when interest rates fall! I should point out here that not only are all the various terms explained within the body of the book, but they are also defined in the glossary at the end.

Someone asked me the other day about how the bond market worked. I have been asked that question countless times, but this time, without a lot of forethought, I blurted out, "It is all about relationships." After I said it, I realized that I had tripped over the most concise and accurate description of how the bond market actually functions: relationships. Your success in the fixed-income market will be directly related to your relationship with your IA. Therefore, I spend some time discussing how to find a suitable one. That IA will have to have an excellent relationship with the trading desk of his or her firm. And that trading desk will have to have a strong relationship with all the IAs of that firm, as well as with the various trading counterparties it trades with. Thus, I stress the value of finding the right IA, one who will provide you with a good financial relationship and who knows how to build a relationship with the bond trading desk of his or her firm.

In addition — and this is vital to your understanding of the fixed-income markets — almost all bonds trade in relation to another bond. Most bonds do not trade every day, so they are priced in relation to a bond that does. You will discover that bond prices change all the time, all day long, as the actively traded bonds (dubbed "benchmarks") change in price. Other factors that can affect your returns are the relationship between short-term yields and long-term yields (the "yield curve"), the yield relationship among developed countries, the relationship between supply and demand in the different sectors of the market, and the relationship between today's prices and yields and historical prices. This, in turn, permits you to conduct technical analyses, which can be of great help in timing purchases and sales. I urge you to study all these relationships, as they are vital to understanding this gigantic, practically invisible market.

I will also share with you some of my personal thoughts, experiences, and anecdotes from a lifetime in the securities business. I have held a wide variety of positions, including research analyst, institutional bond trader, institutional salesman, zero coupon specialist, portfolio manager for two prominent financial organizations (Standard Life and Investors Group), and global bond trader for CIBC. Since 1988, I have built and managed three fixed-income trading departments whose mission was (and still is) the provision of competitive pricing on a complete array of fixed-income products combined with top-notch service to investment advisors and their individual clients.

A ***benchmark bond*** is an actively traded bond that is used to determine the prices of less actively traded bonds. The media report benchmark prices so that the investing public can see the direction of bond prices. As well, issuers of new bonds use them as reference points to price their issues. The Bank of Canada regularly adds to existing benchmark issues at the key maturity dates: two, three, five, ten, and thirty years. This contributes to a smoothly functioning marketplace. Investment dealers also use these benchmarks to hedge market risk.

I will briefly explain the wholesale or institutional business and point out its relevance to the retail market for fixed-income securities; its dominance and structure go a long way in explaining why the retail fixed-income investor has difficulty finding good service and prices. Another important reason for this difficulty is the poor education of both IAs and their clients. I am a leading proponent of making fixed-income markets more visible or transparent to the investing public by electronically distributing a wealth of prices and offerings on an extensive array of constantly re-priced fixed-income products, solely with the retail investor in mind. (I use the term *transparency* to mean the ease with which individual investors can gain access to information and prices for fixed-income securities. Fixed-income trades would be reported post-trade for everyone to see.) These quotations are now made available through IAs or directly to private clients via electronic connection with various vendors such as Bridge, CGI, Reuters, or Bloomberg. The larger investment dealers offer bonds online to their internal sales forces and their discount brokers via their own private legacy systems. There are several initiatives underway in the realm of transparency. The net result will be broader visibility and availability of real-time bond pricing for individuals. Also, these online systems come with tools to make it easier for individuals to implement their strategies. I talk more about transparency later.

Like all markets, the bond market is undergoing a transformation. As governments of all levels have improved their fiscal situations, they issue fewer and fewer bonds, while corporations issue more and more. While the relatively safe government bonds, both federal and provincial, will still be available, there will be a greater selection of corporate bonds and structured notes. The amount of money invested by individuals in Canada in fixed-income investments totals approximately $900 billion. Between one-half and two-thirds of this total is in no-yield or low-yield bank deposits or GICs. Bond mutual funds amount to $147 billion, while investments in individual fixed-income products total approximately the same. It is my belief, and a central theme of this book, that a large percentage of this money will find its way into individual fixed-income products, which, combined with safety of principal, offer greater yield than do bank deposits and GICs. Simply put, bond mutual funds charge too much in fees and produce average returns with uncertain future value. GICs are too short-term for long-term planning and are illiquid. Individual bonds offer a defined income stream, a known future value, liquidity, plus the flexibility to accommodate individual circumstances.

Now, let us begin the process of providing you with the information and tools to help you make financial decisions in your best interest.

CHAPTER ONE
So, What's a Bond, What's the Bond Market, and How Does It All Work?

What Is a Bond Anyway?

It's a piece of paper (well, a computer blip these days) that "bonds" borrowers and lenders. The borrower rents money from the lender and agrees to pay a certain rate of interest for the rental, normally at prearranged times, typically every six months. Thus, a bond is the original amount of the loan plus a series of rental cheques or interest payments. Eventually, the lease is up and the landlord gets the property (capital) back and can re-lease it or hold on to it.

Here is the anatomy of an actual bond, the Canada 5 percent due June 1, 2014. For purposes of illustration we will assume a principal value of $100,000. In other words, $100,000 is the amount that the lender will receive back at maturity. I will use this bond in different chapters of the book. This is a benchmark issue, with $10.867 billion outstanding. This bond pays interest semi-annually, so we may display the internal workings of this bond as follows: the interest payments are the principal value ($100,000) times the coupon rate (5 percent) divided by two, since the interest is paid twice a year. Therefore, each payment is $2,500.

Date	Interest	Face Value
June 1, 2006	$2,500	
December 1, 2006	$2,500	
June 1, 2007	$2,500	
December 1, 2007	$2,500	
June 1, 2008	$2,500	
December 1, 2008	$2,500	
June 1, 2009	$2,500	
December 1, 2009	$2,500	
June 1, 2010	$2,500	
December 1, 2010	$2,500	
June 1, 2011	$2,500	
December 1, 2011	$2,500	
June 1, 2012	$2,500	
December 1, 2012	$2,500	
June 1, 2013	$2,500	
December 1, 2013	$2,500	
June 1, 2014	$2,500	
June 1, 2014		$100,000
	$42,500	

So, an investor who bought and held this bond until maturity, without reinvesting any of the interest payments, would receive a total of $142,500. If the investor held this bond inside an RRSP or held it in a taxable account but did not need the interest, each of these interest payments would need to be reinvested. I am introducing the concept of reinvestment at this stage, as it is a very important component of bond yields. Bond yield calculators assume that each interest payment will be reinvested at the purchase yield, clearly not a real world assumption, but it does provide consistency, as all bonds are measured the same way. Don't worry; we will examine all of this later in more detail.

At one time, investors in bonds received beautifully lithographed letter-sized pieces of paper as evidence that they had made this loan. Today, most of these physical pieces of paper have disappeared, replaced by the "book-based" system, whereby the Central Depository for Securities (CDS) maintains the records of who owns what. Your evidence of ownership is the contract you receive from your financial institution and your monthly statements.

Most bonds are issued with a coupon rate, which is the rate of interest investors will be paid. How is this rate determined? It is a product of the length of time to the maturity date, the general level of interest rates, and the creditworthiness of the borrower. Unlike a mortgage, which is a specific relationship between an individual and a lender, there may be hundreds of holders of the same bond, as individual bond issues may range from $15 million to $20 billion.

What Is the Fixed-Income Market, and How Does It Operate?

The fixed-income market, or bond market, operates in what we call an "over-the-counter" manner. To understand what this means, let us first examine how the equity market functions. When investors purchase, say, one hundred shares of BCE Inc., they purchase them from other investors who are selling the shares at the same price. These trades take place on a public stock exchange where prices are clearly visible. Both the buyers and the sellers pay a fee (or commission) to their respective IAs. The financial institutions (for example, investment dealers or brokers), hereafter called FIs, merely facilitate this transfer from the buyer to the seller; they do not assume any principal position and thus do not risk their principal or capital. Therefore, retail equity transactions are called agency transactions, since the FIs act as agents.

The bond market functions in an entirely different fashion. There is no visible public market, and almost every trade is done on a principal basis and is quote-driven. That is, the FIs' bond traders are using the firms' capital to maintain inventories and make markets in the broad spectrum of fixed-income securities.

Consider BCE for a moment. It has one class of common shares with 926,950,000 shares outstanding as of June 28, 2005. At the same time, it has forty bond issues outstanding, of all different sizes, maturities, and characteristics, ranging in maturity from 2004 to 2054 and in coupon from 0 percent to 11.45 percent. Many of them are held in large percentages by the investing institutions, rendering them illiquid. Very few of these issues trade every day, so if you are interested in investing in one of them, your IA will ask the retail bond trading desk, which will likely not have them and will turn to the wholesale bond trading group, which will then attempt to make a market for that particular bond.

It is somewhat like a grocery store or convenience store. To help individual investors, retail fixed income departments stock their shelves with inventories of the various bond and money market products. There are special sales at times, and of course the investment dealers will showcase the products that they want you to buy. When inventories run out or become low, the retailers go to the institutional department to get restocked. As retailers have all kinds of costs — communications, technology, salaries, rent, and financing the inventories, to name some — prices are marked up from the institutional price. I can tell you that the price markups are very small at most investment dealers. As with grocery stores, you can comparison shop by opening accounts at different investment dealers or discount brokers.

Quotations for bonds often confuse investors. The base denomination for bonds (other than stripped bonds) is $1,000. This is called the "face," "book," or "par" value (we will refer to it as face value for the remainder of this book). It is the principal amount that you invest and will receive back at maturity. We quote bonds on a percentage of face value. When you see a bond quotation it may be, for example, $98. This means that the bond is trading at 98 percent of the face value. In other words, the $1,000 bond is worth $980. As well, bonds (except for stripped bonds) trade with accrued interest attached. The value of that accrued interest is not included in the price. The seller of the bond that you are buying expects, and deserves, to receive the interest accruing from the last interest payment. The buyer pays that accrued interest in addition to the purchase price. This is because the new owner of the bond will receive the full interest payment when it is eventually paid even though he or she is entitled to only the interest accruing from the date of purchase to the settlement date of the sale. Assume, for example, that you sold a bond, there were three months before the next payment, and you did *not* receive the accrued interest. The next owner of the bond would then receive the full six months' interest payment when it came due. Therefore, the next owner's money earned double for that period and yours earned nothing! Since it is impractical and inconvenient to wait until the payment is received before selling the bond, the interest owing to the seller is calculated and paid by the new owner on the settlement date. Let us re-examine the above example: a bond paying 5 percent semi-annually with a face value of $10,000 is sold at 98 percent of face value with ninety days of accrued interest owing to the vendor. The seller of the bond receives $9,800 of the original principal plus the accrued interest owed from the last payment date. If this bond had been held for a full year, the investor would have received $500 in interest (5 percent of $10,000). We divide $500 by the number of days in a year to calculate how much interest accrues daily: $1.3699 accrued per day. Now we take this number and multiply by ninety to arrive at how much accrued interest is owed to the seller: $123.29 of accrued interest. Therefore the seller receives the $9,800 plus the $123.29 of accrued interest for a total of $9,923.29.

> The terms ***bid, ask,*** and ***offer*** create some confusion. When you are selling a bond, the investment dealer provides you with a bid. If you are buying, you need to know what the dealer is asking for the bonds or where he offers it. It becomes confusing when you say that you want an offer for these bonds. That could mean that you want a bid. Stick to bid and ask.

What happens to the buyer?

Assuming the buyer pays the same percentage of face value, he or she pays exactly the same as the vendor receives. In the real world, the two prices will not be the same, but the accrued interest will be. As we recall, the bond market functions as a principal market where the investment dealers make markets in bonds using their firm's capital. Thus, there will be a difference in the "bid," what a trader is willing to pay for a bond, and the "ask," which is the price at which a trader is willing to sell. As well, the IA needs to make a living, so he or she takes the bid or ask price from the trader (depending on whether the client is selling or buying), subtracts or adds the commission, and then gives the client a net price.

Getting back to the buyer, when the next interest payment is due, the buyer will receive the full six-month payment ($250). Subtracting the $123.29 interest previously paid, the buyer has netted $126.71 of accrued interest for the period that he or she has owned the bond. Should this new owner keep the bond through successive payment dates, he or she would receive the full $250 each six months until the bond is sold or it matures.

Also, you will notice that prices for bonds range from discounts, say $90 (or 90 percent of face value), to premiums, such as $110 (or 110 percent of face value). Why is this? Interest rates move up and down, and bond prices move inversely to yields. (Not a week goes by without someone asking me which way bond prices go when yields go up. They go down. Bond prices and yields move in opposite directions, and you will understand why when you read the chapter "Basic Math.") This is to put them in line with currently issued bonds. If the price on our Canada 5 percent bond due June 1, 2014, was exactly $100, then its yield to maturity would be 5 percent. If market yields moved to 6 percent, no one would buy this bond at 5 percent, so we adjust its market price to $93.42, which equates to a yield to maturity of 6 percent. Conversely, if yields fell to 4 percent for this maturity, this bond would be re-priced to $107.15. We will examine in detail how these prices are actually calculated in the chapter "Basic Math." Don't worry.

Individual quotations on bonds (bids and asks) are not readily visible, although there are determined attempts underway to increase the transparency of the bond market. Online or discount brokers have offerings of fixed-income securities, while in the case of FIs, the IAs can see their firms' inventories displayed electronically from their internal systems and can relay these to their customers.

There are daily quotations in newspapers and more extensive lists in the weekend press, but they are not all-inclusive; they typically represent institutional pricing (greater than $1 million in size), and they are just a snapshot at a certain point in time. While they are useful indicators of where bond prices were, bond prices will be different when you attempt to buy or sell, since they fluctuate far more than investors (and IAs) realize. In any event, retail investors will not be able to transact at these prices for two basic reasons: first, they are dealing in retail quantities; second, since the bond market is a principal market, as we now know, a bond trades on a net basis (that is, with no visible commission added).

Let us consider that there might be a different (i.e. higher) price for a retail fixed-income transaction by individual investors than for a wholesale purchase by a giant financial institution. Returning to our grocery shopping analogy, individuals normally find the shelves adequately stocked for their relatively small purchases. If the store did not maintain adequate inventories, the management would have to shuttle back and forth from the wholesale warehouse. The warehouse sells in bulk quantities, so the store manager must decide how much to buy, balancing the needs of the customers with the prices for different quantities of merchandise. After adding the merchandise to the shelves, the manager now raises the wholesale price to retail to account for various factors such as heat, lighting, salaries, insurance, spoilage, and taxes.

A retail fixed-income department operates in a similar fashion. I do not run to the wholesale, or institutional, market for every $10,000 worth of bonds that I sell. Instead, I will sell them "short" (that is, sell now and buy later), or I might suggest another bond that I do have in inventory. In practice, I buy in bulk various fixed-income products from the wholesale market and add them to my "shelves," which I call my inventory. Once I do that, I incur market risk, which I offset by hedging. Hedging involves neutralizing market risk so that I do not incur capital gains or losses as the market prices change. I do incur yield-curve risk and credit risk. I also maintain state-of-the-art computer and communication equipment. As well, there are the other basic costs, such as remuneration! Also, since most bonds do not trade every day, I resort to "matrix" pricing to at least provide a quotation. How do I do that? I do that by comparing one of those bonds to an actively traded benchmark issue such as a Government of Canada bond of similar maturity and adding a yield spread to that bond based on where I know or believe that they have been trading recently, and then I compute a price. It as if I know there are some Bell bonds down in the factory, but rather than keep you waiting, I price them and sell them to you now and go buy them later because I know what my relative cost will be.

Even given all this, the markups from the wholesale fixed-income market to the retail market are amazingly small, meaning that individual investors can be well served by the fixed-income market.

This type of pricing is necessary since, returning to the BCE Inc. example, there may be just one class of common shares outstanding, but there could be thirty or so different bond issues of different maturities, sizes, and features. There is just not enough liquidity to display a bid and an ask all the time in the same fashion as the equity market. The FI "makes a market" in the various instruments, willing to be long or short to accommodate investor interest. In addition, governments of all types borrow money in the bond market, and, of course, they do not have any common shares to trade!

The ***transfer price*** is the price at which the fixed-income trading department transfers bonds to the IAs. To get paid, they must add a commission to this price in the case of an investor purchase.

The bottom line is that the bond market functions as a clearing house between borrowers and lenders. For IAs to earn a living, in the case of client purchases, they raise the ask price received from the bond department and get paid the differential as a commission. This is not visible to the investor. The opposite occurs when clients sell, with IAs deducting from the bond desk's bid to create a commission.

Furthermore, the less-liquid bonds, such as corporates and zero coupons, are most frequently quoted on a matrix basis. Since many of these instruments do not trade every day, they are priced in reference to an instrument that does. For the most part, Government of Canada bonds of different key maturities constitute the benchmarks by which other securities are priced. While I have included more on benchmarks later, I think it is important to mention them now, as the majority of fixed-income securities offered to investors are priced in relation to them. The Bank of Canada is committed to building up very large and therefore liquid benchmark issues at the key maturities: two, three, five, ten, and thirty years. They are vital not only in pricing bids and offerings, but also in pricing new provincial and corporate issues when they come to market. The benchmarks form a valuable base level from which other bonds may be valued. For example, let us take a provincial bond: the Province of Ontario 5 percent bond due March 8, 2014. It is valued by the market at 20 basis points above the relevant benchmark, the Canada 5 percent due June 1, 2014. To trade these, a trader will observe where the Canadas are trading, add the 20 basis points to the benchmark yield, and then calculate the price for the Ontario bond. Let us say that the Canada 5 percent June 1, 2014, is trading at $107.43 to yield 4 percent. Now we add the 20 basis point spread and arrive at a yield of 4.2 percent for the Ontarios, which produces a price of $105.75.

Thus, as the liquid, actively traded benchmark issues change in price and yield, so do all the matrixed bonds. The yield spread between the benchmarks and these bonds fluctuates in reaction to supply and demand factors, changes in the yield curve, and changing credit risk perceptions.

The role of investment dealers, then, is to make markets in a wide-ranging list of bonds, bidding for bonds for which there are no apparent buyers or short-selling bonds where they are not sure there are sellers. FIs sell bonds short all the time, either to accommodate demand when they know there will be a seller of the same bond soon or to hedge long positions (quantities of bonds that they already own). They may also short-sell bonds if they think they have become expensive compared with some other bond. Thus, they are a buffer between the differing needs of a cross-section of bond market participants. These longs and shorts are all held in the dealers' inventories, which are typically segregated by type (money market, short-term Canadas, mid-term Canadas, long-term Canadas, provincials, strips, and corporates). The dealers hedge these inventories with offsetting transactions in the benchmark issues (or in the futures market) to eliminate or reduce market risk. Bond trading volumes are enormous, averaging approximately five times the daily amount of equity trading (approximately $23.5 billion). Why is this? First of all, the amount of bonds outstanding is huge, exceeding $1 trillion in Canada.

Corporations and governments issue bonds all the time for various reasons, such as rolling over maturing debt, paying off bank lines, funding deficits, and building new factories. Investors of all kinds (governments, pension funds, mutual funds, trust companies, life insurance companies, foreign investors, and individual investors) all have varying fixed-income needs, and these needs change over time. Some of these investors trade for speculative reasons, others think they can outsmart their peers by aggressive trading, while still others merely match the term of their assets and liabilities. In addition, new issues come to market that may be more attractive than bonds already owned. As well, bonds mature, making money available for reinvestment, or as

Composition of Canadian Fixed-Income Markets
(As at May 31, 2005, $billion)

Money Market (less than one year)		
Treasury bills	federal	$ 125.20
	provincial	$ 13.00
Bankers' acceptances		$ 34.60
Commercial paper		$ 119.40
Total money market		$ 292.20
Bond Market		
Federal government bonds	domestic	$ 391.40
	foreign	$ 12.90
Provincial and municipal bonds	domestic	$ 298.20
	foreign	$ 112.90
Corporate bond	domestic	$ 213.10
	foreign	$ 208.10
Total bonds:		$1,236.60
Grand Total		**$1,528.80**

Note: Stripped bonds of $87 billion included.
Source: Bank of Canada

Trading Volume First Quarter 2005 Daily Average
($billion)

Money Market	
Treasury bills	$ 5.61
Bankers' acceptances	$ 4.93
Commercial paper	$ 9.51
Total money market	$20.05
Bond Market	
Canadas	$20.78
Crown corps, provincials, and municipals	$ 1.75
Corporates	$ 0.53
Strip bonds	$ 0.45
Total bonds	$23.51
Grand Total	**$43.56**

Source: IDA

they shorten in term over time investors may wish to sell them in order to buy ones with a longer term to maturity.

What Does the Bond Market Look Like?

The bond market is largely invisible, being decentralized, over the counter, and with no post-trade disclosure. It resembles an onion with a series of layers. At the heart of the Canadian bond market is the Bank of Canada, which is in charge of monetary policy and open market operations in the foreign exchange, money market, and bond market.

Next come the money market "jobbers," whose role is to ensure the orderly maintenance of the money market, including the issuance of Government of Canada treasury bills. The money market is defined as securities issued with a term to maturity of one year or less. Treasury bills are obligations issued by the various governments. They are issued at a discount from their face value and mature at their face value so all the yield is in the amortization from that discounted amount.

Primary dealers for bonds:

BMO Nesbitt Burns, Inc.
Casgrain and Co., Ltd.
CIBC World Markets Inc.
Deutsche Bank Securities Ltd.
Merrill, Lynch Canada Inc.
J.P. Morgan Securities Cda. Inc.
Laurentian Bank Securities Inc.
National Bank Financial Inc.
RBC Dominion Securities Inc.
Scotia Capital Inc.
The Toronto Dominion Bank

Then we have the primary dealers, many of whom are also jobbers. Among other things, they are required to bid for the auction of the Government of Canada's primary bond issues. They do the bulk of the underwriting of new provincial and corporate debt, make markets in the complete array of fixed-income products, and service the fixed-income needs of the various institutional and retail investors by maintaining extensive inventories and bidding and offering on all sizes of blocks of bonds. Individual trades can be in the hundreds of millions or for as little as $5,000. The lion's share of the daily $23.5-billion trading volume takes place among the Big Six investment dealers (at the time of writing, they were RBC Dominion Securities, TD Securities, CIBC Wood Gundy, BMO Nesbitt Burns, Scotia Capital, and National Bank Financial) and their institutional and global customers. The market for individual investors is approximately 5 percent of this total. The other 95 percent is in the institutional area, where the bank-owned dealers (plus a few non-bank-owned dealers, such as Merrill Lynch Canada, Desjardins Securities, and Casgrain and Co.) make wholesale markets in all the various fixed-income products to serve the investment needs of their institutional customers. These customers include life insurance companies, chartered banks, pension funds, mutual funds, investment counsellors, governments, and foreign investors. It is worth pausing to note that the money that these institutions have for investment represents the aggregate savings of individuals like you! Your money is mixed in with everyone else's, thus giving the institutions very large sums of money to invest and trade. A large percentage of this money is invested in fixed-income securities to satisfy actuarial requirements, match liabilities, and guarantee fixed returns. With large blocks of money to invest, these institutions command and receive the best prices. The investment dealers vie for this business: competitive tendering for bids and offerings is the norm. Individual trades exceeding $100 million are commonplace.

Naturally, all of the bank-owned dealers serve individual investors since they all have national sales forces of IAs. There are another 205 members of the Investment Dealers Association (IDA) who transact fixed-income securities. There are large, independent firms such as Blackmont Capital, Canaccord, and GMP Capital as well as a host of small and medium-sized investment dealers such as Watt, Carmichael, Altus Securities, Odlum Brown, Haywood Securities, and Dundee Securities. Each of these firms has to find fixed-income products somewhere in order to satisfy their customers' needs. The bank-owned dealers help to meet these needs. They offer, via electronic delivery, retail quantities and prices of the various fixed-income products. TD Securities, Merrill Lynch, and RBC Dominion Securities are prominent in this area. Also, a company called CollectiveBid aggregates prices and offerings from a number of contributors and makes them available to all these same small dealers and entities. Blackmont Capital has also begun to offer its fixed-income inventory to a number of these dealers.

Several of the larger independents, such as Blackmont, Dundee, Canaccord, and Odlum Brown, have their own specific fixed-income trading departments staffed by experienced personnel. They have sufficient capital and technology resources to assemble, maintain, and offer a wide range of fixed-income securities to meet the needs of their IAs' customers. Blackmont Capital, for example, has a department of four professionals who have enough capital to maintain inventories of approximately $100 million. They manage these aggregates on a fully hedged basis to eliminate market risk for the firm and to offer competitive prices at all times. With an online, real-time trading system at their disposal, they can offer their own inventory plus fixed-income securities that they do not own. This is possible owing to the presence of actively traded, large bond issues for which there exists a known market. Knowing what spread they trade at in relation to one of the benchmark issues makes it easy to offer a security without owning it. In fact, the benchmark prices are fed electronically into this system as they change, ensuring that the IAs' customers are always seeing live prices. Also, in a typical sales force, some clients are selling securities that others will be buying. Knowing this, the trading department will keep and hedge the sold securities for later resale to its own sales force rather than to "the street," the large market-making investment dealers mentioned earlier. This is an efficient way to do business, and customers benefit through better prices. Running to and from the wholesale market for every small transaction is very expensive.

Yet that is what the smaller dealers must do as they do not have the personnel or capital to keep an inventory themselves.

It is also worthwhile pointing out the different philosophies of the various investment dealers with respect to how they treat individual fixed-income investors. Most of the bank-owned dealers treat their retail customer base as a captive audience and therefore charge more for individual bonds than the smaller, more focused firms. What you need to know is whether the FI you are dealing with treats the retail fixed-income market as a profit centre or not. The best ones work at growing the business through value-added service and competitive prices. Make a point of ascertaining what approach your FI uses.

Also, there are interdealer brokers whose role is to act as middlemen, facilitating anonymous trades among the jobbers, primary dealers, and investment dealers. These parties trade among themselves to offset transactions done with clients.

Lastly, we come to the individual investor whose needs are served by the different FIs. Individuals have their own specific reasons for purchasing fixed-income products directly: to generate income, to plan for retirement, and to provide safety of principal. They may need income in a foreign currency, they may wish to speculate on the price movement of bonds, or they may want to invest some money for future educational needs. Direct investment by individuals in the bond market totals in excess of $100 billion. In fact, if GICs and bank deposits are included, this total increases to more than $900 billion.

The Case for Bonds

Why go through the bother of purchasing individual fixed-income securities? Why not take the easy route and invest in a nice bond mutual fund? The answer to the second question is that it is not in your best interest to do so! Mutual bond funds simply do not offer the certainty required in retirement planning; their performance is erratic, and the management fees are too high. I speak from experience. For five years I managed what is now the largest mutual bond fund in Canada.

Sadly, there are too few IAs with sound enough working knowledge of fixed-income markets. The line of least resistance for them is to recommend bond mutual funds because they are an easier sell and the fees are attractive. However, they are not the ideal choice for the individual investor. Here are five reasons to choose individual fixed-income products.

Planning. Fixed-income products have specific maturity dates. That is, you know the exact date at which your principal will be returned to you and what your yield will be for the term that you hold this security. Contrast this with bond mutual funds: They do not have a specific maturity date, nor do they have a specified income level. Investors do not know what their investment will be worth at any moment or what it will be worth when they actually need their money back. Bond fund managers are constantly tinkering with their portfolios, shortening term, extending term, and trading for capital gains. This is not conducive to effective planning.

Fees. Bond funds charge management fees averaging approximately 1.8 to 2.0 percent per annum! This takes a serious bite out of an investor's income and return. Contrast that with individual products, where there is a one-time fee at the time of purchase (averaging 1 percent) with no further fees until they mature and the money is reinvested or if they are sold before maturity.

Performance. The long-term results of "professional" bond fund management are not impressive, for a couple of reasons. First, it is a well-documented fact that no one is 100 percent sure of where interest rates are going. All forecasters, traders, and market commentators are right some of the time, but nobody is right all of the time. However, this does not stop portfolio managers from guessing using a technique with the more elegant name "rate anticipation trading." It only takes a couple of bad guesses for performance to suffer. Second, there is indexing in the bond fund management business too, as brave portfolio managers huddle around the different bond indices in order to look good in the performance game and earn those bonuses for their professional management. They strive to beat the index as well as more than half of their peers so they will be able to market above-average performance. Also, consider that bond funds are required to calculate an annual return since they do not have a fixed maturity date. Investors owning individual bonds do not have to worry about annual returns since their yield and maturity date are known at the time of purchase. A good analogy is a baseball game. Individual investors in specific fixed-income securities know the outcome of the game before it starts even though the score (the annual return) may vary by inning. Bond fund holders have to worry every inning since they may have to leave the stadium before the end of the game without knowing the outcome.

Maturity selection. Bonds come in a wide range of maturities, from thirty days to more than thirty years, allowing for appropriate retirement planning and ladder building. Bond funds do not have a maturity date so investors do not know how much money they will have when they need to redeem their units.

Liquidity. Bonds can be sold at any time, should raising money become important or should other opportunities present themselves. Daily trading volume averages some $23 billion, with the major investment dealers maintaining bids and asks on the complete array of fixed-income products that have been issued. Mutual funds can only be redeemed daily.

Bond Indices

There are several bond indices in the Canadian bond market. One of the most widely used for bonds in Canada is the BIGAR™ (Broad Investment Grade Analysis of Return) Composite Total Return Index, which is produced by CIBC World Markets. This index encompasses some nine hundred different bond issues and is constantly being rebalanced so that it fairly represents the overall bond market. As of June 30, 2005, it consisted of 48 percent in federal bonds, 26.1 percent in provincials and municipals, and 25.9 percent in corporates. The corporates are further weighted by credit rating. The average duration was 6.38 years. *Duration* is a term that refers to the average term of the bond, taking into account the weight of the interest payments. Thus, duration is shorter than the term to maturity and is a measurement of the volatility of a bond. More on this later.

For the twelve months ending June 30, 2005, this index returned 11.85 percent while Canadian-managed bond funds returned a median of 9.4 percent. This gap is partly explained by the fees charged to the fund by the manager. This is called the management expense ratio (MER), which averaged approximately 2 percent in this period.

What to do then? I referred in the introduction to a strategy called laddering, which is fully explained later. Suffice it to say here that laddering takes the guesswork out of interest rates, reduces fees, and, over time, outperforms the majority of bond fund managers. This is done with individual fixed-income securities of staggered maturities. Basically, it is the most effective way of dealing with reinvestment risk, as your investments are spread out over regular intervals. This approach eliminates the need to guess which way interest rates are going, as investing in bonds of different maturities avoids the risk incurred if all your funds were invested in one maturity and interest rates were very low when that investment matured. There will be more on this important method in Chapter 6.

It is in your best interest to take control of your financial future by arming yourself with the knowledge of how to invest in individual fixed-income products. Doing this will offer you greater certainty as to the future value of your money and cost you less in fees.

CHAPTER TWO
So How Do I Get Started?

It is likely that you already have a relationship with an FI and/or an IA. It may be a bank, a bank-owned investment dealer, an independent brokerage firm, a mutual fund company, a financial planning company, a life insurance company, or a trust company. All of these entities, through their IAs or agents, first attempt to sell you their products, even if they are not suitable for you. Very few IAs (my guess is 10 percent) actually have your best interests in mind. Therefore, you will have to arm yourself with all the knowledge you can and find an experienced IA to act for you.

Your IA's firm will have lots of educational material available, and there are a plethora of websites to help you along. I have included this list in Appendix A. These websites offer all kinds of analytical tools. The daily newspapers offer some commentary, and television shows such as CNBC and ROBTV have expert commentators on a regular basis, including me. There are books available, and your IA's firm will likely offer daily, weekly, and monthly bond market commentary. Over time, all of this information will stand you in good stead as you will have a good knowledge base.

So, armed with all this knowledge, you should be able to get your broker/advisor to do what you want, shouldn't you? Not necessarily! Each pillar of the financial services industry (banks, trust companies, mutual fund companies, life insurers, investment dealers, and advisors/planners) has a vested interest in selling you what is in its best interest, not yours. Rare is the organization (or individual) that actually listens well enough to ascertain the needs of the client and takes care to make sure those needs are met, even at the expense of a sale that might produce greater near-term reward.

How and where do you find such people? The number one method is referral, from an IA's satisfied clients or from lawyers, accountants, and friends. Ask, ask, ask, and eventually you will find someone who will help you. At some point, you will likely receive what are called cold calls. These come from IAs just starting out who are trying to build their books. It is in your best interest to find IAs with experience and well-established books of business so that you are well served. It is possible that you may not find such IAs or your account may not be large enough for them. The major investment dealers offer superb training for new IAs, which includes the fixed-income markets. Therefore, you may find a newer IA who might be suitable for you, but remember to ask, ask, ask.

IAs' ***books of business*** refer to how many clients they have and what the assets of those clients total.

So How Do I Get Started?

This market remains a decentralized or over-the-counter market. With myriad issues to choose from and with mammoth trading volume and institutional dominance, it becomes extremely important to select the right firm and then the right advisor. The choice of a firm must be made before you pick an advisor. Extra time spent on this decision can mean significantly enhanced returns and thus a higher standard of living and more comfortable retirement.

The first step is to determine whether an investment dealer or organization takes the retail fixed income business and its participants seriously. Look for FIs who advertise a special focus on fixed-income needs. Develop basic questions to ask would-be financial advisors. Here are some common questions, as well as the answers you should be looking for.

Q: "Is the retail fixed-income desk a captive of the wholesale desk or is it master of its own destiny?"

A: To properly serve individual investors, the retail fixed-income desk should be focused on providing IAs and their clients with good advice and competitive pricing.

Q: "Is it a stand-alone profit centre or is the desk's compensation linked to the overall growth of the firm's fixed income business?"

A: A desk that is motivated to grow the business of the IAs will offer the best overall service.

Q: "What percentage of your business is fixed income?"

A: It should be in the 20 percent to 50 percent range.

Q: "How is the bank rate set?"

A: You should be told it's set at regularly scheduled meetings of the Bank of Canada (bankofcanada.ca).

Q: "Assuming I have $100,000 in my RRSP, what kind of fixed-income portfolio would you recommend in individual securities?"

A: IAs should mention stripped bonds (zero coupons), corporate bonds, and the concept of laddering, and should not suggest bond mutual funds.

Q: "What is the difference between semi-annual and annual yield?"

A: It depends on the level of nominal rates. It is an important question, since GICs, for example, are quoted in annual yield terms while most bonds are offered in semi-annual terms. Most firms will convert one to the other for fair comparison. It is in your best interest to ensure that you are being offered an apples-to-apples comparison, since annual yields may appear to be higher than semi-annual yields when, in fact, they may be the same or even lower.

Q: "How much commission do you charge on bond trades?"

A: If they answer at all, it should be between 0.5 percent and 1 percent.

Q: "Do you know what duration is?"

A: This is important as it represents the risk and volatility of a bond. It is the average term of a bond, including the interest payments.

Q: "What is the size of your book and how many clients do you have?"

A: A minimum size of $50 million and perhaps 250 clients would indicate a successful IA and one who, therefore, would not need to do frequent transactions to make a living. Ask if they are willing to do a price comparison test with other FIs. It may not be easy to get these answers, but persist. Ask friends, read the financial papers, listen, observe.

Q: "If I find the right advisor, how easy or difficult is it to move my account from my existing financial institution?"

A: Naturally, FIs are not keen to see customers leave and so they do not make it easy to do so. In days gone by, it was a genuine hassle to move your account. Now the rules have changed and your account must be moved, in cash or kind, within days or the FI faces fines. It also helps that almost all securities are book-based, so this transfer becomes a simple matter of a computer transfer — plus the inevitable paperwork, of course. The FI that you are moving to will expedite the transfer. To move your account, first open a new account with the new FI. Once that is done, complete, with the help of your new IA, a Request for Transfer Form, which serves notice to your former firm that you would like to transfer your account. The former firm must reply to this notice within two days and deliver all the securities and cash within ten days. For a complete description of this process, visit www.IDA.ca and look in the Investor Education section.

The advisors you are seeking are not likely to be rookies. They will probably have more than ten years of experience with a large, balanced book of clients. They will be working for an FI that has a comprehensive inventory of individual fixed-income products and a variety of tools to make your investing easier. Most major FIs have websites replete with prices, calculators, portfolio-building strategies, and, of course, offerings of all the various products.

There are also an increasing number of institutional bond salespeople who, late in their careers, become retail advisors. They can be of immense assistance to the individual investor given their knowledge of the entire fixed income spectrum, as well as their ability to take advantage of how the bond market functions. If you are talking to a branch manager of an FI, ask if there is an IA there who specializes in fixed-income products or has a strong knowledge of and client base in these products. Typically, IAs with only a passing knowledge of bonds are timid and unsure in approaching the trading desk personnel, who, to such IAs, appear to be a bunch of fast-talking, untrustworthy types. Unsure of themselves and of how to interact with the market, they may shy away. However, skillful handling of the information, services, and expert personnel of the typical well-staffed fixed income department by a person steeped in the knowledge of how this market functions can produce measurable rewards for fortunate clients. Knowledgeable IAs will have access to bargain lists and will know of important economic releases and the upcoming borrowing calendar. These IAs are well placed to add income and yield to your portfolios. The experienced advisor also gains the respect of the traders, lets them know what his or her specific areas of interest are, and thus gets calls when specific offerings appear.

Following are some representative questions and comments that IAs will use with their bond trading department.

Q: "My client can buy those bonds cheaper somewhere else."

A: This is a loaded one; most of these apparent discrepancies can be explained because this is not an apples-to-apples comparison. In other words, the client (or IA) may be comparing the identical security, but one yield may be quoted in annual terms and the other one in semi-annual terms. At 5 percent this difference is 6.25 basis points even though the price is the same (see the chapter on basic math). As well, the comparison may be hours or days old, and bond prices do change minute by minute. The securities being compared may not be exactly alike; there may be slight differences in maturity, credit, or features that may affect the relative yield between different fixed-income products. Another explanation could be that another investment dealer is offering a special sale. Worse yet, advisors may be trying to get a lower transfer price (the price at which the trading department transfers bonds to IAs). This is the IAs' cost and they add a markup to earn a commission. If they do obtain a lower price from the trader, that improvement is not necessarily passed on to clients. Needless to say, traders become wise to ploys such as these and handle the offending parties appropriately.

The relevance of this is that it is an over-the-counter market and there are inefficiencies. Clients may receive, or say that they receive, better prices from another FI. It may be because one IA is charging more commission than the other or that one firm's bond desk is running a special on a certain bond. It does underscore the point that the more experienced your IA is, the better the treatment you will receive.

Q: "Why can I not buy this bond at the same price as quoted in the weekend newspaper?"

A: This is a very common question. The newspaper quotations are snapshots of market prices at a particular instant, typically 4:00 p.m. the previous business day. They are quotations representing only the market for transactions larger than $1 million and before any brokerage or commissions are added. The large lists of bond quotations in, for example, the weekend *Toronto Star* or the *Globe and Mail* are matrix-priced, meaning that each bond is not priced individually but in relationship to the benchmark issues. In such cases, there is no allowance for any idiosyncrasies or features of a bond that could affect its price. What happens is that a keen client, eager to learn the ways of the bond market and therefore studiously following everything, discovers a few really high-yielding bonds in the weekend paper and phones an IA Monday morning to scoop up these bargains before those slow-moving bond traders catch on. The advisor, of course, smelling a sale, rushes to the bond desk asking for offerings without a shred of thought. In almost every case, these bonds have certain features — usually call features —

nean that the issuer may redeem those bonds before maturity and ıdvertised yield in the newspaper may not be realized. (The papers m..., not have the inclination or the space to show the yield to call.) In addition, the issue may also be small, a private placement, in the hands of foreigners, or the whole issue could have been stripped with no public float at all.

Q: "My client just inherited $350,000. What do I do?"

A: A good retail fixed-income desk will ask the IA more questions as to quality and maturity preferences and then construct a customized portfolio. If an IA just recommends a bond fund, then this IA is not doing his or her job.

How to Get Along with a Bond Desk

I have seen all aspects of human behaviour in managing retail fixed-income trading desks. I have built and managed two retail-oriented fixed-income trading desks since 1988, and I am now building a third one for Blackmont Capital Inc. The first was for Dean Witter Canada, which was eventually sold to Midland Walwyn, which got taken over by Merrill Lynch, whose retail arm was sold off to CIBC Wood Gundy, where many of the Dean Witter IAs had come from when Wood Gundy got out of retail. What a business! The second one was for First Marathon Securities, which needed a retail-oriented bond trading desk to service the fixed-income needs of its rapidly growing Correspondent Network, which today clears and trades for a very large number of financial organizations: some small investment dealers, some large ones, some investment counselling firms, and some investment subsidiaries of very large FIs. First Marathon was purchased by the National Bank in 1999 and merged with Lévesque, Beaubien. NBCN became the abbreviation for the National Bank Correspondent Network. I am now in the process of building another retail-focused fixed-income trading desk for Blackmont Capital Inc., an independent investment dealer focused on the individual investor. It is owned by Rockwater Capital Corporation. To all of our IAs, my department offers a complete array of fixed-income securities via an online, real-time order entry system. We also offer customized portfolio design, market commentary, and research. As well, we offer fixed-income securities to some of the more than two hundred IDA members that do not have their own inventories.

Each of these trading desks has had the same philosophy — to be in charge of its own destiny and to be driven and compensated primarily by the growth in the retail fixed income business. In this way, IAs know that their bond trading desk is served by helping their business to grow.

On the one hand, I have observed thoughtless, short-term-oriented IAs adversely affecting clients' returns while alienating the trading desk at the same time. On the other, I have had the pleasure of working with enlightened, informed, intelligent, long-term-oriented IAs who reap huge benefits for their clients by adroit use of the market and the desk. No more than 10 percent of any sales force falls into this latter category — hence my focus on selecting the right advisor.

I have seen and heard it all: IAs looking for an ask when they really wanted a bid; strange trades initiated at month end with the sole motive of generating commission; outright lies (e.g., saying XYZ broker is offering something cheaper); pleading for a lower price only to keep the difference and not pass the savings on to the client; apples and oranges comparisons, days or hours apart; confusing annual and semi-annual yield; yelling and screaming when the price cannot be matched or has changed. To a person, these IAs say they cannot trust the desk and are getting ripped off, when really it is they who are hurting themselves and their clients through this time-wasting, counterproductive behaviour.

Trading desks make or take a thousand calls a day and execute more than a thousand trades per day. They know what they are doing, what the prices are right now. Some IAs attempt to outsmart them; what they should be doing is being straight with them, and they will receive the same treatment in return. IAs should also be spending more time with their clients. I am always amazed when an acquaintance tells me that not only does he not understand what his money is invested in, but that he does not see his advisor routinely, perhaps once a year at best! At stake here is the return to the client, as consistently bad behaviour makes us leery of certain IAs, and therefore their clients will suffer.

Contrast this with informed IAs who realize that the desk is on their side — at least a tool for them to use, at best an active partner in helping improve their business. They trust the traders and realize that there are bargains to be had at different times, as well as (with the market knowledge of the desk) assistance in timing purchases to again help clients achieve superior yield. These astute IAs are more aware of pending release times for important, market-moving news and new-issue timing. With proper desk contact, IAs learn of temporary sell-offs or rallies to take advantage of. Trusting the desk or at least being straight with it yields huge advantages. Contrast this with the mistrustful IAs who play petty games with the traders, getting their backs up. In fact, through frequent communication with the desk, IAs may pick up gratuitous tips or advice to further their clients' (and their own) after-tax standard of living.

You want to seek out an IA who has a sound working knowledge of the fixed-income markets and who does a high percentage of business in fixed income. Listen to the IA describe how he or she gets along with the desk; if it's not mentioned, ask. The answer will reveal a lot. Human nature is important; traders are human and will respond favourably to professional treatment. Of course, trading desks are not perfect. One mistake or misunderstanding in an over-the-counter market may colour one's opinion for a long time. However, a quick glance at the commission statistics will reveal in almost every case that the IAs who give the desk a hard time are in the lowest quartile of production. They waste too much time playing games with the desk and not enough time taking care of their clients. The top quartile of producers do not waste their time or the traders' time through childish antics. Every retail organization where I have worked has these IAs. It is the same as with a lot of other businesses, where 20 percent of the IAs do 80 percent of the business. You want to find one of those IAs. The other 80 percent complain and play games and just waste too much time on unimportant issues.

Transparency, Transfer Prices, Markups, and Commissions

One of the main reasons — if not the main one — why investors either do not know enough about fixed-income markets or are too timid to venture into them is the lack of transparency of this giant market. As we have discussed, there is no central location for the bond market. Instead, it operates on an over-the-counter, decentralized basis. There is no ticker tape showing trades as they take place, nor is it easy to obtain a quotation.

The investment dealers make their markets in bonds using their own capital, unlike the stock market, where most trades occur on an agency basis (buyer and seller meet and a transaction takes place without the investment dealer needing to use capital).

Why does this difference exist, and what is being done about it? First of all, the majority of the outstanding fixed-income issues do not trade every day, with the noticeable exception of the very liquid Government of Canada benchmark issues. Quotations on almost all other bonds are calculated on a matrix basis, where a certain bond is priced in relation to benchmark issue of a similar maturity. Otherwise, how would investors know what to pay for an illiquid bond? At the same time, the daily retail fixed-income transactions are estimated to number between five thousand and eight thousand, with an estimated face value of $500 million, perhaps 5 percent of the total market. This implies an average individual transaction size of between $60,000 and $100,000. These trades all happen privately as each investment dealer has its own private electronic delivery system for providing bids and offerings on a complete spectrum of fixed-income instruments to its IAs and then to their customers. Discount brokers also display offerings in a similar fashion, providing online tools to assist investors in selecting issues, building ladders, and calculating yields. Each system is different, and there is no public display of the trades.

In the meantime, a company called CollectiveBid has developed and introduced a fixed income system that features several contributors (Merrill Lynch, HSBC, J.P. Morgan, Laurentian Bank, CIBC World

Markets, and Casgrain and Co.) showing retail bids and offerings to a growing list of smaller investment dealers. While it offers good software and reasonable offerings, it has one weakness: of the Big Six investment dealers, only CIBC World Markets has become a contributor. These dealers see no reason to do so and remain content to distribute their fixed-income products internally to their captive sales forces.

There are more than two hundred IDA members and only eight or so retail-oriented trading desks to service them all. What are the Big Six doing? For one, they created a company called CanDeal, which exists to make markets electronically in the most active Government of Canada issues, but only for institutional customers. It was modelled after a company called TradeWeb in the United States that is now trading approximately 30 percent of U.S. Treasury bonds online. Recently, the Toronto Stock Exchange made a $20-million investment in CanDeal, signifying its interest in this business and perhaps staking out a possible future role as central consolidator for the fixed income business.

Where is this going? In the huge American market, only a handful of electronic bond trading platforms remain after there were once more than one hundred. Only two are profitable.

In Canada, it is hard to imagine more than one system surviving in each of the institutional and retail spaces. It is equally difficult to imagine why the Big Six would want to give up their private monopoly over their own sales forces and clients. Gradually, inexorably, some veils will be lifted, but there will be stout resistance from institutional bond traders, loath to share any trade information with rivals. There is a system in the United States called TRACE (the Trade Reporting and Compliance Engine for corporate bond transactions). It broadcasts, with a delay, the last sale price and other relevant trade data for U.S.-dollar-denominated, investment-grade, and high-yield corporate bonds. The delay was at the behest of the major investment dealers, who argued that immediate dissemination of corporate bond trades would put them at a competitive disadvantage. The bank-owned dealers are advancing the same argument in Canada. We are nowhere close to such a system here.

Transparency is a long way off, but retail investors will have more choices and more tools.

Where do I stand on this? I am in favour of greater transparency for individual investors in fixed-income securities for the simple reason that the more investors can see a market, the more they will trade in it. As a trader, that means more trading volume, and that is a good thing! I also think some sort of post-trading reporting system showing at what prices bonds actually traded would help lift at least one veil from this over-the-counter market.

Much of the pressure to reveal more has to do with markups and commissions. Let us first reexamine the process. The major investment dealers maintain extensive inventories, using their own capital to do so. They incur hedging costs to minimize risk and make large investments in market-making systems, communications, and back-office infrastructure. There are spread risks, yield curve risks, and credit risks. This helps explain why there is a spread between the bid and the ask sides of a market, with that spread representing the risks associated with bidding for that particular bond. For example, when bidding for an obscure corporate bond, traders must take into account its credit rating and the likelihood of finding a buyer for it. They may own it for months, and the bid will reflect that. Conversely, bidding on an actively traded Canada issue is simple because they know they can sell it right away.

When it comes to the retail offering of bonds, each trader takes all of these risks into account and offers the inventory to the sales force at what is called the transfer price, which is the price at which the trader will transfer the bond to the IAs. There is no commission built in; this is merely the traders' ask price. As this is a principal market, the IAs need to add a markup to this price to earn a commission. It is this markup that is the hot button for the regulators. Investors see how much commission they pay when trading equities, but not so when buying fixed-income securities (including GICs). Investors pay a 1 to 1.25 percent commission when buying a five-year GIC.

My opinion on this, after managing retail fixed-income trading desks for fifteen years, is that most fixed-income trades are done with fair markups. There have been — and no doubt there still are — some rogue IAs who take excessive markups, but they are the exception. Every investment dealer has internal guidelines for markups, and offenders are penalized. The marketplace enforces discipline, as it is possible to check prices with other dealers. Each investment dealer generates an up-to-date list of transfer prices on a complete spectrum of fixed-income instruments. These prices are not much different in practice from one fixed-income trading desk to the next. The different prices that clients pay for the securities arise mostly from the different markups charged by IAs.

Let us go through an example. Assume an investor wishes to buy $50,000 Province of Ontario 5 percent of March 8, 2014. The transfer price is $107.75 for a yield to maturity of 3.93 percent.

Transfer price: $107.75
Yield: 3.93 percent
Markup: $1.00
Total price to client: $108.75
Yield: 3.81 percent
Amount client pays: $50,000 * $1.0875 = $ 54,375.00
(expressed another way, the client is buying fifty $1,000 bonds priced at $1,087.50 each)
Transfer cost to IA: 50 * $1,075.00 = $53,875.00
IA's commission: $500, or almost 1 percent.

This is a typical commission for such a bond. At shorter maturities, the yield is affected more for a given markup, so markups are typically lower for, say, one- to five-year maturities than they are for the longer maturities. Also, markups typically become smaller as the size of the transaction increases. My recommendation for an investor with a large sum of money to invest is to ask two or more investment dealers for competitive offerings. Knowing this, the IAs at these firms will reduce the markup in order to win the transaction. On a trade of $250,000 a markup of 0.5 percent would be typical, for a gross commission of $625.

Let us now consider stripped, or zero coupon, bonds. They are a rarity in the investment business, as they are excellent products for retirement planning while they offer higher percentage markups for IAs. Let us assume that the same $50,000 was going to be invested in an Ontario stripped bond of the same maturity and at the same yield. The transfer price on the Ontario 0 percent March 8, 2014, at a yield of 3.93 percent, is $71.29.

Transfer price: $71.29
Yield: 3.95 percent
Markup: $1.00
Price to client: $72.29
Yield: 3.77 percent
Amount client buys: $50,000 / .7229 = $69,165
Transfer cost to IA: $69,165 * .7129 = $49,307
Amount client pays: $69,165 * 0.7229 = $49,999.00
IA's commission: $692.00, or 1.4 percent

Again, this is a typical markup and is common throughout the business. It is not an outrageous amount, especially when you consider this is a one-time fee for what most likely will be a buy and hold situation. In any event, these fees are in line with what IAs charge for equity transactions, in the region of 1 to 2 percent.

Remember, GIC investors pay a markup, too, as the issuing agents pay the investment dealers $1 to $1.25 at the five-year maturity.

The hue and cry over fixed-income market markups is somewhat misguided. This is a self-policing business and a competitive one. I think it is reasonable for IAs to make a reasonable living. Investors may ensure that they are obtaining fair prices by opening accounts at more than one investment dealer or at a discount broker. Having at least two accounts at separate FIs will ensure favourable pricing, especially when you have one with an IA at a full-service firm. Investors are advised to obtain competitive quotations, especially for large transactions, say over $100,000. IAs who repeatedly attempt to overcharge will find their business declining. When contemplating a fixed-income transaction, let your IAs know that you are requesting at least one other quotation. This keeps them on their toes, and they may consider lowering their markups. Should you not do this, it is standard behaviour for an IA and an FI to take advantage of a monopolistic situation.

CHAPTER THREE
Basic Math

What you'll want to remember: present value = future value / $(1 + r)^t$

It is no wonder that the investing public has a difficult time comprehending the bond market when they are told that bonds are issued in denominations of $1,000 but are priced out of $100. This $1,000 is the principal amount, or face value. Adding further confusion is that bonds are priced as a percentage of this amount, as we saw earlier.

While the minimum unit of a bond is $1,000 face value, the pricing out of $100 actually makes it easier to understand when you realize that a price of, let's say, $98 represents 98 percent of the face value of the bond, which by extension, makes one bond in this example worth $980. It is an uphill struggle, but one must remember that bond traders are simple folk and pricing out of $100 is easier.

What Is a Basis Point?

This is a phrase commonly used in the fixed income business and one that I use frequently in this book. Consider what 1 percent in yield represents. Most bonds do not trade at round yields such as 3 percent, 4 percent, or 5 percent. Even though they may have been issued with those yields, once they start to trade, their yield moves up and down and so they will be presented in fractional form. For example, if interest rates move upwards by one-half of 1 percent, a bond issued at 5 percent will be quoted as yielding 5 1/2 percent. Seems simple enough. However, most of the time, the yield will not fluctuate so evenly and so you might find this same bond quoted to yield 5 37/100 percent. This is a little unwieldy, so what the simple bond folk have done is to divide 1 percent into one hundred even pieces, each one of which is called a "basis point." In bond lingo, basis points are known as "beeps." Thus, 25 basis points constitute 25/100, or 1/4 of 1 percent. The bond people then replace fractions with decimal points. So, if a bond moves up in yield by one basis point, they do not quote it as yielding 5 1/100 percent but rather 5.01 percent. The previous example of the bond moving up by 37 basis points would therefore be quoted at 5.37 percent. Got it? It is important to remember the definition of basis points, as that is what we use to compare one bond with another. For example, the Ontario 5s of 2014 yield 20 "beeps" more than the Canada 5s of June 1,2014: 4.20 percent versus 4.00 percent.

This chapter is about mathematics, money, and yield. Money invested earns a return. If money is invested in bonds or other fixed-income investments, the return consists of regular interest payments plus the ultimate return of the original amount loaned. If the interest is not needed, it will be reinvested, thus earning interest on interest, a concept we label *compounding*. This is a key concept that we'll return to later.

The first concept we will discuss is *present value*. Understanding it will lead you to the full knowledge of how to correctly value a bond or, at least, to fully understand the concept of present value (and which way bond prices go when interest rates go up).

Obviously, $100 today is worth $100 today; it has no time value. Would you lend someone $100 today for, say, two years, and accept nothing but the $100 back? Unless this was a family member or an extremely close friend, you would likely ask for some interest on the loan; otherwise you would have loaned your money for nothing. Money has time value. Putting it another way, $100 due in two years is not worth $100 today — not unless it were to earn 0 percent and inflation were zero. In the real world, money earns a return and there is inflation, so in two years, $100 will grow by the amount of interest (both simple and compound) earned during that period. The present value formula calculates the present value of that future amount of money using a discount rate, or yield. This concept is vital to a solid understanding of how the bond market functions and is extremely important to retirement planning. That's why I included it at the beginning of this chapter. Here it is again: present value = future value / $(1+r)^t$, where r is the interest rate per period and t is the number of periods.

Do not despair! Present value tables have already been prepared for your ease of use and enjoyment. I have included such a table in Appendix B.

To determine the current value of $100,000 due three and a half years from now at a semi-annual yield of 5 percent, you would calculate the answer thusly: $100,000 / (1+2.50 percent)^7 = $100,000 / 1.02750^7 = 1/1.18868.60 = $84,126.52. Stated differently, $84,126.52 today invested at 5.0 percent compounded semi-annually will grow to $100,000 in three and a half years.

Before continuing, we will spend some time discussing compound interest, since the all-important present value is merely the reciprocal of a compounded amount.

Compound Interest

Baron de Rothschild described interest as "the eighth wonder of the world." Interest compounds, which is a concept vital to the understanding of yield to maturity. Compounding means that not only does your original dollar earn interest but interest you receive also earns interest by being reinvested. In this case, we are compounding on a semi-annual basis; although this appears to complicate matters, the domestic bond market functions on a semi-annual basis. Thus, a bond paying semi-annual interest and paying 5 percent pays that 5 percent in two payments of 2.5 percent each, paid six months apart. The following example will use an original face value of $100,000. This amount will be returned at maturity, in this case three and a half years from now. There will be seven interest payments made. How much will each payment be? The original face amount times the interest rate divided by two: $100,000 * .05 / 2 = $2,500.

Interest	Compound Interest	Total Interest	Amount	Total
$2,500.00	$ 0.00	$ 2,500.00	$100,000.00	$102,500.00
$2,500.00	$ 62.50	$ 5,062.50	$100,000.00	$105,062.50
$2,500.00	$126.56	$ 7,689.06	$100,000.00	$107,689.06
$2,500.00	$192.23	$10,381.29	$100,000.00	$110,381.29
$2,500.00	$259.53	$13,140.82	$100,000.00	$113,140.82
$2,500.00	$328.52	$15,969.34	$100,000.00	$115,969.34
$2,500.00	$399.23	$18,868.58	$100,000.00	$118,868.58
$17,500.00	$1,368.58	$18,868.58	$100,000.00	$118,868.58

We will assume that all of these payments (except the last one, since it is paid at the same time the $100,000 is repaid) will be reinvested or compounded at the same rate (2.5 percent) for the remaining term of the investment, and so on with each successive payment. This might be a difficult concept to grasp initially, but it is how bond calculators work. It provides a common yield measuring device for us simple bond folk, since it is obviously not a real world calculation. In the real world, every interest payment will be invested at a different yield, if reinvested at all.

Thus, $100,000 invested today at 5 percent compounded semi-annually will grow to $118,868.58 in three and a half years.

Explaining this table in more detail, the first interest payment of $2,500 is received after six months. At twelve months, the next $2,500 is paid, but since the payments are being reinvested, the first $2,500 payment will have earned 2.50 percent, or $62.50, during those six months; this is the interest on the interest, or what we call compound interest. For the next payment, the $2,500 is received plus the interest earned on the first two payments plus the compound interest ($2500 + 2500 + 62.50) * .025 = $126.56. So, the total is now the three payments of $2,500 each plus $62.50 plus $126.56, for a total of $7,689.06, and so on, until the compounding period ends and the total future value totals the original face value plus the interest payments received (7 * $2,500 = $17,500) plus the total compound interest of $1,368.58: $100,000 + $17,500 + $1,368.58 = $118,868.58.

Let us now go back to the present value formula since it will be referred to many times and it is a very important concept. Since the previous calculation shows the future value of a sum invested today at a certain interest rate for a specified period of time, we should be able to calculate the present value of a sum in the future discounted by an interest rate for a specified period of time. All we have to do is take the reciprocal of the future value formula. In other words, $118,868.58 discounted at an interest rate or yield of 5 percent semi-annually for three and a half years is worth $100,000 today. If you wished to express this out of a round amount like $100,000, simply divide the $100,000 by $118,868.58 and get an answer of .841265. Thus, $84,126.50 invested today at 5 percent semi-annually compounded will grow to exactly $100,000 in three and a half years. This calculation is very important when we discuss stripped bonds in a later chapter. A present value table calculated for a wide number of terms to maturity and interest rates may be found in the stripped bond chapter. There is also a more complete present value table in Appendix B.

Let us now move to a real bond, the Canada 5 percent bond, maturing June 1, 2014. This is a benchmark issue with some $10.867 billion outstanding. We will demonstrate how the value of this bond is really determined by calculating the present value of each of the interest payments and the principal. For this example we will assume a yield or discount rate of 5 percent for each of the components and that the bond was bought at a price of $100, which we know is 100 percent of face value. In addition, we will assume that the bond was purchased on December 1, 2005, so that the first payment is in exactly six months. You can calculate all these present values yourself by using a present value table, the calculator found on my website (www.inyourbestinterest.ca), or Excel, which has bond math in its Analysis Tool Pack.

I am assuming a cost of $100 for a semi-annual yield of 5 percent as of December 1, 2005. Price per $100 is therefore $100, exactly the cost of the bond.

Date	Coupon Face Value	Principal	Discount Rate	Present Value of $1	Payment Value
June 1, 2006	$2,500		5.00%	0.97561	$ 2,439.03
December 1, 2006	$2,500		5.00%	0.95181	$ 2,379.53
June 1, 2007	$2,500		5.00%	0.92860	$ 2,321.50
December 1, 2007	$2,500		5.00%	0.90595	$ 2,264.88
June 1, 2008	$2,500		5.00%	0.88385	$ 2,209.63
December 1, 2008	$2,500		5.00%	0.86230	$ 2,155.75
June 1, 2009	$2,500		5.00%	0.84127	$ 2,103.18
December 1, 2009	$2,500		5.00%	0.82075	$ 2,051.88
June 1, 2010	$2,500		5.00%	0.80073	$ 2,001.83
December 1, 2010	$2,500		5.00%	0.78120	$ 1,953.00
June 1, 2011	$2,500		5.00%	0.76214	$ 1,905.35
December 1, 2011	$2,500		5.00%	0.74356	$ 1,858.90
June 1, 2012	$2,500		5.00%	0.72542	$ 1,813.55
December 1, 2012	$2,500		5.00%	0.70773	$ 1,769.33
June 1, 2013	$2,500		5.00%	0.69047	$ 1,726.18
December 1, 2013	$2,500		5.00%	0.67362	$ 1,684.05
June 1, 2014	$2,500		5.00%	0.65720	$ 1,643.00
June 1, 2014		$100,000	5.00%	0.65720	$65,720.00
Total	$42,500				
Grand Total	**$142,500**				**$100,000.53**

As you can see, a bond is merely a sum of its parts; put another way, yield to maturity is the discount rate that equates the future cash flows to today's price.

Now you see how artificial the yield to maturity calculation is, since yields at different maturities will not be identical. Put another way, the odds of each coupon payment being reinvested at the purchase yield are very, very, low. For that to be the case, yields would have to be the absolute same at all the interest payment dates as at the time of purchase. We will see when we discuss yield curves that this is a very rare event. Another calculation produces the realized yield, which takes into account the effect of different reinvestment rates on the yield to maturity. This calculation is best left to calculators. What you need to remember is the longer the term of the bond, the more important the interest payments and, therefore, the more important the interest on the interest.

Following is an example of a longer-term bond, the Canada 5.75 percent due June 1, 2029. Showing the effect of different reinvestment rates illustrates how important interest is when assessing the value of a bond. These numbers represent the total amounts received if this bond was held to its maturity date with the reinvestment rate varying. The importance of reinvestment rates is also striking. In all three cases, the interest received over the life of the bond exceeds the final principal repayment.

Canada 5.75% June 1, 2029

	4.28%	5.75%	10.00%
Principal	$100,000	$100,000	$100,000
Interest Payments	$138,000	$138,000	$138,000
Compound Interest	$ 98,888	$151,828	$402,573
Total	$336,888	$389,828	$640,573

"Thrift is a wonderful virtue — especially in an ancestor," said Mark Twain. Compound interest is one of the strongest forces in the investment business and one of the keys to investing success. For example, the following table indicates how long it takes for $1 to double at different semi-annual compounding yields (pre-tax, of course).

Rate	Years to Double
4 percent	17.5
6 percent	11.7
8 percent	8.8
10 percent	7.1
12 percent	5.9

You may have noticed that multiplying the rate times the number of years produces an answer close to seventy-two. The "Rule of 72" says that if you divide seventy-two by the interest rate, the answer is the number of years (approximately) that it takes for money to double.

So you want to make a million? The present value of $1 million due in twenty years discounted at a yield of 10 percent semi-annually is $142,000. Therefore, $142,000 invested at 10 percent will equal $1 million in twenty years (pre-tax, but this is possible in RRSPs). At 5 percent that same $142,000 would grow to only $381,279 in the same period, while at 15 percent it would grow to $2,562,281! These dramatic differences underscore how important it is to take advantage of high yields when they are available. At 8 percent compounded semi-annually, $1,000 will grow to more than $2,000 in nine years, $7,106 in twenty-five years, $50,504 in fifty years, and $2,550,749 in one hundred years.

You can see that compounding is a very powerful force. Consider the tale of the numerically naive king and his mathematical daughter who happened to be a whiz at checkers. He offered her monthly prizes for scholastic achievements. His daughter told him that she wanted just one dollar to be put on the first square of her checkerboard after the first month and then to have that amount doubled every succeeding month. So, on month two it would be $2 on the second square, $4 on the third month, and so on, until the sixty-four squares were full. Well, the king ran out of money. By the tenth square, he put down $512, and by the twentieth, it had become $524,288. The amount would have been in the trillions by the time he reached square sixty-four! She was earning a 100 percent return per month.

Reinvestment Risk

It is vital that after gaining the knowledge of how important compound interest is, investors understand how much their future retirement stakes are at risk. There are two types of reinvestment risk: interest rate risk and maturity risk. The first has to do with the risk of reinvesting interest payments at lower interest rates than existed at time of investment, and the second means having too much of your portfolio invested in one maturity, exposing yourself to the possibility of having to reinvest most or all of your money at lower interest rates.

Let us again review the concept of yield to maturity of a bond. On a typical semi-annual bond, the quoted yield to maturity assumes that each and every interest payment is reinvested at that yield. They would have to remain constant at the purchase yield for the entire life of that bond! This is not likely in the real world, since interest rates are dynamic; yields are rising and falling all the time. So, this yield to maturity calculation is artificial. As we have seen, the longer the term of the bond, the more important the total interest received. For example, a 5.75 percent bond paying semi-annually and due in 24 years will produce 1.38 times in simple interest payments and 1.52 times in compound interest the original principal amount, assuming a constant reinvestment rate of 5.75 percent. Look at the Chart of the 5.75 percent June 1, 2029 on page 58, which underscores the importance of this reinvestment rate.

Since a quoted yield to maturity on a bond is far removed from the real world, you might wonder why this yield calculation is done at all. It offers a consistent way to value all bonds and helps in valuing one bond in relation to another one. Investors are at greater risk than they realize unless they are invested in a product with no reinvestment risk. Yes, Virginia, there is such a product, and it gets its own chapter later on: the zero coupon or stripped bond. To combat this reinvestment risk, I advocate a laddered portfolio (involving staggered maturities) of stripped bonds in an RRSP account, as stripped bonds have no interest to reinvest. I advocate the laddered approach for taxable portfolios as well. More on this later.

The other form of reinvestment risk involves maturity selection. In day-to-day terms, planning your retirement with short-term investments is like timing a marathon runner after 100 yards and extrapolating the result over the ensuing 26 miles, 285 yards. The following high-tech chart outlines the direction of interest rates since the Second World War:

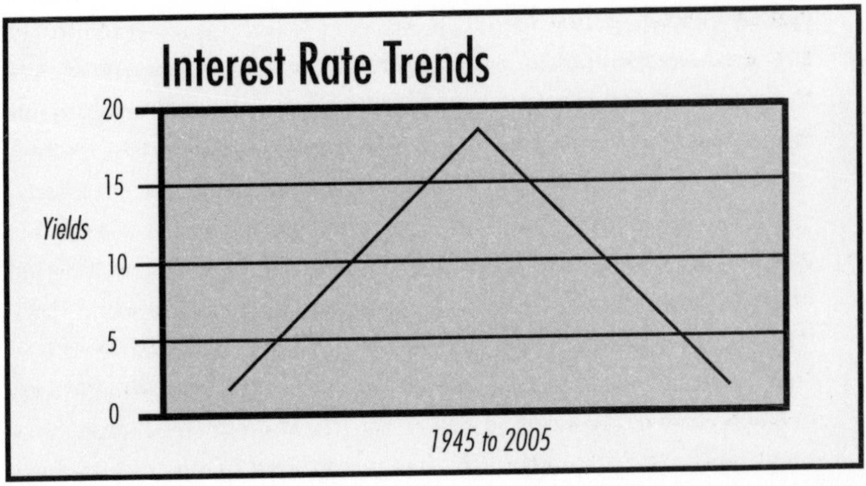

While somewhat simplified, it underscores the reinvestment risk of maturity selection. No one knows where interest rates are going, so why take a chance? Since the peak in yields in 1982, anyone who has invested retirement funds in treasury bills and GICs has discovered the unpleasant experience of having a high-yielding investment mature with much lower yields available.

Historical Yields

Year	Five-year GICs	Long-Term Canadas
1982	16.14%	16.33%
1987	8.79%	8.51%
1992	7.92%	8.92%
1997	4.91%	7.38%
Today	2.50%	4.30%

As you can see, five-year GIC rates have moved progressively lower. In 1982, you could have invested in a twenty-year Government of Canada bond at 16.33 percent. Buying the five-year GICs and renewing for five years when they matured produced progressively lower returns. In fact, very few investors are aware of their complete investment choices since they are never told what they are; they are "sold" investments deemed suitable for them by their IAs that are not in their best interest.

For a typical RRSP plan, the previous table underscores the long-term effects of investing in short-term investments at a time of declining yields. I am writing this book in such a period. Obviously, in a period of generally rising rates, staying short is a winning process since yields will be higher as each bond matures. The purpose of this chapter is to stress the fact that, since even the great Templeton has not found anyone who can consistently forecast the trend in interest rates, it is important to find an approach that removes or significantly reduces reinvestment risk. It is the laddered approach, and it is fully discussed in Chapter 6.

Since the domestic bond market is built around semi-annual yield and the issuers (banks and trust companies) of deposit instruments (GICs, mainly) typically quote their yields in annual terms, it is important to know the "apples to apples" comparison, since the difference can be meaningful.

Consider a one-year investment of $100,000 offered at a yield of 5.0625 percent annually and compare this with another one-year investment paying 5 percent semi-annually. Which one would you buy? On the surface you would buy the one yielding 5.0625 percent, but assuming we invest $100,000 in each of them, let us see what they return:

	Annual 5.0625 percent	Semi-annual 5 percent
Interest (6 months)	$ 0.00	$2,500.00
Interest (12 months)	$5,062.50	$5,000.00
Compound Interest	$ 0.00	$ 62.50
Total Interest	$5,062.50	$5,062.50

Thus, we can say that 5 percent compounded semi-annually is equivalent to 5.0625 percent annually. Obviously, the higher the yield, the greater the difference:

Semi-Annual	Annual Equivalent
4 percent	4.04 percent
5 percent	5.06 percent
6 percent	6.09 percent
7 percent	7.12 percent
8 percent	8.16 percent
9 percent	9.20 percent
10 percent	10.25 percent

Investment advisors worth their salt will provide both yields so there can be no misunderstanding. Since this is not typically the case, and since investment products are seldom offered at a nice round yield, how can you work this out yourself? You could use a simple formula. To convert from semi-annual to annual, take the semi-annual yield and square it, then divide by four to calculate the number of basis points to add to arrive at the annual yield equivalent. Taking 10 percent semi-annually and squaring it produces 100, and dividing by 4 produces 25 basis points, which when added to 10 percent produces 10.25 percent annual yield equivalent.

For a semi-annual yield such as 7.56 percent, follow the same process: 7.56 squared equals 57, then divide by 4 to equal 14.3 basis points, which added to 7.56 percent produces an annual yield equivalent of 7.703 percent.

Yield, or What You See You May Not Get

Yield is what an investment returns to an investor, whether expressed as dividends, capital gains, interest, or compound interest. As the compound section indicates, the rate at which money or capital grows is crucial to investment results. This brings us to the yield on bonds. Investing in a bond paying 5 percent produces 5 percent a year in interest payments, whether payable semi-annually or not. If that interest is used or spent, a simple yield of 5 percent (pre-tax) is realized. When the interest is reinvested (say in an estate, an RRSP, etc.), then this yield becomes a different matter. When you buy a fixed-income security that offers a 5 percent yield to maturity, it implies that every interest payment will be reinvested or compounded at 5 percent to produce that yield. This is not a real-world calculation. It is merely a benchmark number to measure different bond yields: you may calculate it by buying appropriate software or downloading it from your FI. Or you could get it free from my website. The formula for converting the price of a bond to its yield to maturity is a long, iterative formula best left to calculators. Calculating the price of a bond given its yield is far easier, as it involves adding up all the present values as we have seen.

Duration, or What You See Is Not What You Have

A ten-year bond is a ten-year bond, right? Sorry! The term or maturity of the bond may be ten years, but it would only have a duration of ten years if that were the only payment you received. Returning to the Canada 5 percent due June 1, 2014, we observe that there are seventeen interest payments spaced six months apart plus the return of the principal. These payments are a part of your bond, and since they range in term from six months to nine and a half years, they have an impact on the average life or average term of your investment. Yields and bond prices move inversely. Perhaps I should take a minute and explain that last sentence. Not a week goes by without someone asking if bond prices go up when yields or interest rates go up. After working through the present value calculations, you can see that if interest rates rise, then the present value of the pieces of the bond will be worth less and therefore the total value of the bond will fall. The converse is equally true. If yields fall, the present value of all the parts of a bond rise and the total value of the bond rises.

The same applies for present values of future payments: the higher the discount rate or yield, the lower the present value (and vice versa). Let us take the June 1, 2010, interest payment for example. At 5 percent, as we have seen, this payment has a present value of \$2,001.82. Suppose we raise the discount rate to 11 percent. The present value now works out to be \$1,544.07. Lowering the discount rate to 2 percent produces a higher present value of \$2,285.85. Thinking about it logically, and reversing the formula, at a higher yield, you need less capital today to arrive at a specified future value (and of course the converse is true for a lower yield). Thus, to produce \$2,500 in five years at 2 percent you need \$2,285.05 today, but if you could invest at 11 percent you would need only \$1,544.07.

Each of the payments of a bond has a present value, and taking their relative weights into account along with the present value of the principal payment produces an average life or term of your bond (the average time it takes to receive all the cash flows or payments). This calculation is referred to as the duration of the bond. In our example, the average duration works out to be 7.10 years at a yield of 4 percent. Duration is not static: as time passes, the terms of all the payments become shorter and so does the duration. As well, changes in market yields will affect the present value of the payment stream and thus affect the duration. Let us assume we have a 10 percent bond and a 5 percent bond, both with a term to maturity or principal repayment of ten years. Which one has the shorter duration? The present value of the interest payments from a 10 percent bond will have greater value than those from a 5 percent bond at the same yield. Using a face value of \$100,000, a starting yield or discount rate of 5 percent, and the interest payment at three and a half years produces the following:

Interest Payment	Present Value
10 percent bond:	\$100,000 * 0.10 / 2 = \$5,000 **at 5 percent** = \$4,206.33
5 percent bond:	\$100,000 * 0.05 / 2 = \$2,500 **at 5 percent** = \$2,103.16

The interest payments from the 10 percent bond have greater present value than those from the 5 percent bond, and so the 10 percent bond will have a shorter duration. In this case the 10 percent bond has a duration of 6.3 years, versus 7.8 years for the 5 percent bond. Another way of looking at this is to look at the present value of the two payments above. Each of the interest payments for the 10 percent bond will have a greater present value than will the same maturity interest payment for the 5 percent bond. Adding all the present values up will show that the weight of the interest payments is greater compared with the principal payment for the higher coupon bond, and this will produce a shorter average term or duration.

The reason for stressing this calculation becomes evident when selecting bonds. Duration is used as a measurement of risk. The longer the duration of a bond, the larger the price change for a given yield change. Thus if you believe that interest rates are trending lower, you would invest in bonds of long duration. IAs worth their salt will know what duration is and which bonds are appropriate for you. A shorter duration bond is less sensitive to yield changes.

The following illustrates how duration affects the price change of bonds of different maturities and durations. What I have done is take bonds of different coupon rates at two different maturity dates (five and twenty years) and measured the impact of a 1 percent (100 basis point) shift in the yield from 6 percent to 5 percent. Within the two maturities, the durations change depending on the coupon rate.

Coupon	(years)	Duration in Price	% Increase
Five-year bonds			
	12%	3.9	4.01
	8%	4.2	4.20
	6%	4.4	4.40
	0%	5.0	5.00
Twenty-year bonds			
	12%	10.6	10.90
	8%	11.4	11.80
	6%	12.4	12.60
	0%	20.0	21.50

You can see the bigger price changes for lower coupon bonds of the same maturities. I included a zero coupon bond at each maturity to show that without any cash flows, these bonds have a duration equal to their maturity and have the greatest price change.

Bond Price Dynamics and Volatility

Why do bond prices change? After all, there is a fixed level of interest payments and a final repayment of principal. So what is the point of reporting price changes for bonds daily? The daily trading volume for bonds is enormous, averaging $23 billion, or some five times the volume of the stock market. Various participants in the bond market have reasons to trade their fixed-income investments. The price of money changes frequently, as anyone who borrows or lends money knows. The reasons for this are numerous, including the changing supply and demand for money as the economic cycle changes, changes in the rate of inflation, government deficits, political turmoil, foreign exchange crises, or changes in interest rates in other countries. As well, someone investing in a bond may have circumstances change and need to sell it before maturity. Investors' expectations or inflation or other factors may also change. As well, a large pool of speculative capital trades the bond market aggressively, seeking capital gains. Time is also a factor. Consider someone who buys a ten-year bond. Five years later, that investor has a five-year bond, and new ten-year bonds may be offering a much higher yield, prompting the investor to consider exchanging the five-year bond for the ten-year. There are a whole slew of institutional portfolio managers who are constantly analyzing the market for inefficiencies and arbitrage opportunities. They will examine relationships among thousands of bonds. For example, they may decide that the spread between ten-year Canadas and Ontarios has become too wide based on historical analysis and their own projections and thus they would sell the Canadas and buy the Ontarios, with the aim of reversing the trade if and when the yield spread narrows. Constant analysis by portfolio managers everywhere leads to an efficient market most of the time, but as with all markets, surprises occur. Astute analysts stand to benefit from knowing when there is an anomaly between two different bonds or sectors.

How Do Bond Prices Change and How Volatile Are They?

The following are the basic rules of bond price volatility. Bond price volatility increases as:

The maturity lengthens. Typically, as maturity lengthens, duration does too, and we already know that the longer the duration of a bond, the more its price will change for a given yield movement.

The coupon rate declines. Again referring back to duration and assuming two bonds of identical maturities, one with a 10 percent coupon and the other with one of 5 percent, the latter one has a longer duration and therefore more volatility since the present value of its interest payment stream is not as great as that of the 10 percent bond.

The starting yield increases.

Let us ensure that we are all familiar with the basic tenet of bond prices and yields. Bond prices and yields move in an inverse pattern; that is, as interest rates or yields rise, the price of bonds falls (and vice versa). The longer the maturity, the greater the price movement for a particular bond. Remember the dinosaur.

Imagine yourself on a schoolyard teeter-totter. One end of the teeter-totter represents bond prices, the other end, yields. If someone larger than you jumps on the yield end, it will go down and you will go up to the highest level (price) that the teeter-totter will go. That is what happens to long-term bonds. If you are a little chicken and sit closer to the centre of the board and the same large bully jumps on, what happens? You do not go as far.

The following table illustrates this teeter-totter effect.

Yield Decrease	Price Increase* 3-year	5-year	10-year	30-year
-0.50%	1.40%	2.20%	3.80%	7.30%
-1.00%	2.80%	4.40%	7.80%	15.50%
-1.50%	4.20%	6.60%	12.00%	24.60%
-2.00%	5.60%	9.00%	16.40%	34.80%

*Assuming a 6% coupon and a starting yield of 6%

The Yield Curve: The Shape of Things to Come

The yield curve compares time and yield by connecting a series of dots indicating the yield at different maturities. Practical-minded investors would expect that the longer the term they are willing to lend or invest their money, the higher the return or yield they should receive. The higher yield compensates the investor for the extra risk in lending for a longer period of time. Translating that into a graph would produce the following:

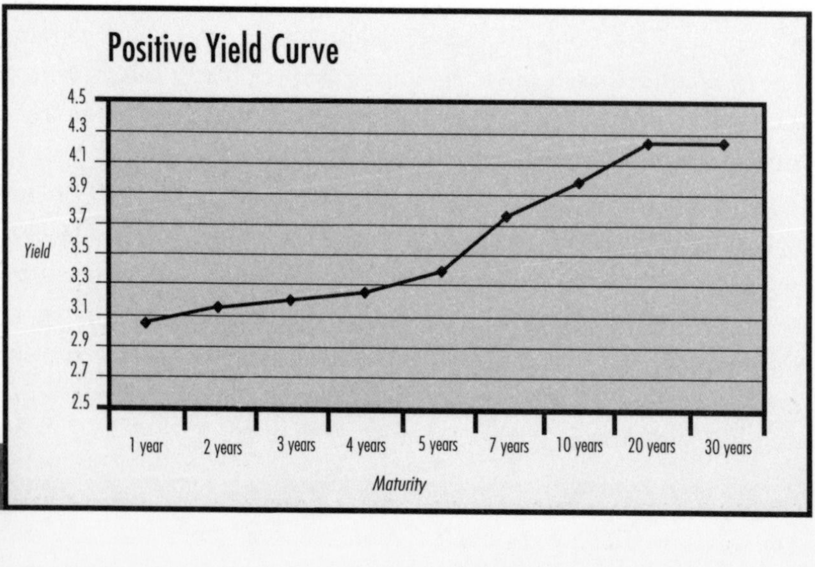

Of course, this curve is not constant; it may be steeper, that is, the upward slope may be more vertical, with long-term yields sharply higher than short-term yields. It could also be flatter, with only gradual increases in yield along the curve. (Note: All the curves in this chapter represent yields available in benchmark Government of Canada obligations, the reference points for all other securities.) The yield curve assumes different shapes at different times in the economic cycle. It can be flat, with yields identical at all maturities:

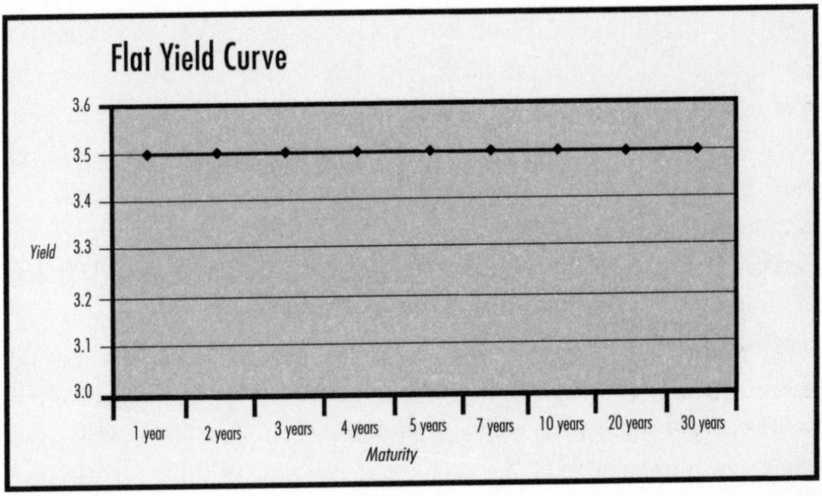

Or it can be inverted, with the shortest maturities offering the highest yields and the longest maturities the least:

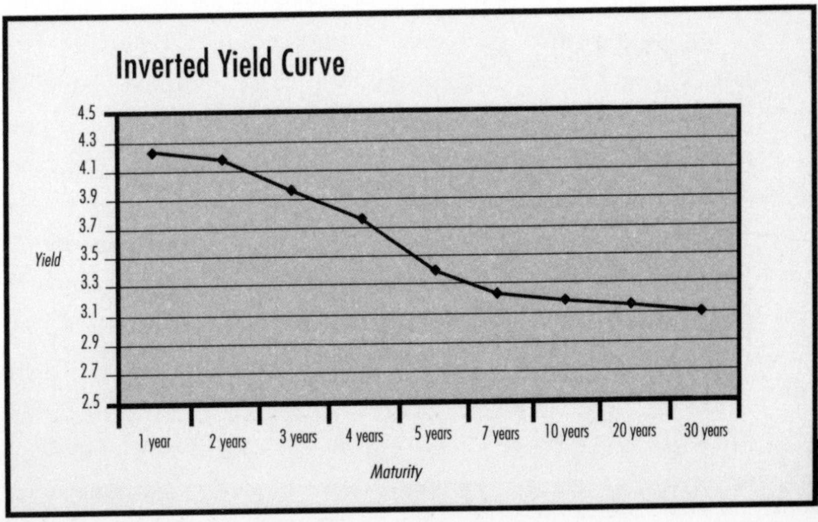

You can draw your own. On a piece of paper, draw a vertical line and a horizontal line. Using the daily newspaper or your favourite website, find the yields at the shortest maturity for Government of Canada instruments (say, three months) and, using the horizontal axis for time and the vertical for yield, place a dot where each yield belongs. You could use maturities such as six months, one year, two years, etc., all the way to thirty years. Then connect all the dots to view your curve.

Why dwell on this? What do these shapes mean? How do you get from one shape to another? What's in it for me? These are all good questions. Dwelling on this increases your awareness of where Canada (in this case) is in its economic cycle. The shapes and the changes in them assist in this analysis. When the yield curve moves from very steep to less steep, it is a sign that the Bank of Canada (or the market participants) believes that it is an appropriate time to be tightening monetary policy, which is a fancy way of saying that the economy needs to be cooled down before inflation gets out of hand. Some observers liken this approach by central banks to taking away the punch bowl when the party gets going. What is in it for you, then, is that you will have an important gauge at your disposal to be used when contemplating decisions such as whether to stay floating with your mortgage or to fix it and whether to buy long-term or short-term bonds. To acquire a good working knowledge of the importance of yield curves is to understand interest cycles, to get along without an economist, and to enhance long-term returns.

The yield curve is dynamic, with the yield relationship between one maturity and another in a constant state of flux. Why is this? For one thing, changes in the shape of the yield curve represent changing inflationary and economic expectations of market participants. At one end of the curve (the very short maturity end) is our central bank, the Bank of Canada, whose duties involve the maintenance of a stable currency, the conduct of monetary policy compatible with economic growth, and a vigilant, anti-inflationary stance. The Bank of Canada may deem it necessary to tighten monetary policy, restricting the growth of money supply and raising short-term interest rates. It can thus be responsible for pushing up treasury bill yields and the prime rate, but can it directly affect long-term bond yields and mortgage yields? The short answer is no. Beyond the shortest of maturity dates, the Bank of Canada cannot dictate where interest rates go. This is because market participants of all types, borrowers and lenders alike, combine to set market rates. For example, when the Bank of Canada begins to raise short-term interest rates, market participants may view this as anti-inflationary and thus they may feel more comfortable investing in longer term securities, whose yields then fall. This is one way that the yield curve flattens (short-term yields rise even as long-term yields fall). This happened in the first half of 2005; you should note that the yield curve remained positive during that time, indicating that the Bank of Canada did not really tighten monetary policy seriously.

At the outset there are a few theorems to advance. Almost always invest in the longest-term investments (for your particular circumstances) when it costs you the most in current income to do so. For example, ten-year bonds may be yielding 6 percent while ninety-day treasury bills yield 8 percent. This inversion of yields normally occurs at a time of maximum monetary tightness, close to interest rate peaks. When rates begin to fall, superior total returns are obtained from investing in long-term securities even though treasury bills appear to yield more. The converse of this is equally true. An investor should invest in the shortest maturities when it again costs the most in current income to do so, that is, when the yield curve is in an extremely steep configuration. In this case, ninety-day treasury bills may be 2 percent and long-term yields 6 percent. This typically occurs at a time of maximum monetary ease by central banks, when the economy is expanding rapidly and is beginning to generate inflationary pressures and when credit demand is strong. At times like this, the next major event is monetary tightening when the central bank begins to ratchet interest rates higher. Interest rates begin to rise at all maturities, so even though current income is higher in long-term investments, total returns will be worse. Your capital is at risk. In other words, capital preservation should become more important at cyclical extremes than extra current income.

One of the principal driving forces of all markets is greed. By always being greedy and reaching for higher apparent yields, investors in fixed-income products may find only short-term benefits. For instance, in the first case above, once the monetary tightening ends and inflation subsides, short-term and long-term rates will both fall. When the ninety-day treasury bill matures, ninety-day bills might then be only 4 percent while ten-year bonds may have fallen to 5 percent. Now the investor must decide whether to take the lower yield on the bills or invest in the ten-year bond at 5 percent that they could have bought at 6 percent. An opportunity lost. The converse is typically true in the other example. After a long period of monetary ease, the Bank of Canada decides to tighten monetary policy and yields rise, so that investors reaching for higher yield at the longer maturities see their principal value decline while short-term yields begin to rise.

In a coming chapter, I discuss the laddered approach to fixed-income investing, as it takes the guesswork out of the equation. Suffice to say for now that it spreads your fixed-income investments over a variety of maturity dates. Until everyone is converted to ladders, it is important to pay attention to both the shape of the yield curve and how it is shifting. It is educational, and it demonstrates that greed (seeking higher yield) may be a false economy if in reaching for that apparent higher yield, investors are putting their principal at risk. A similar analogy is the GIC investor who never considers anything else beyond five years when, in fact, there are times when significant gains in total returns are possible through purchasing bonds of ten- and twenty-year maturities.

In the practical advice section, I mention that a large percentage of investments become concentrated in the one-year and five-year terms. This has a lot to do with the whole GIC business, where one- and five-year terms are most common and so that is where the bulk of term matching takes place, as institutions constantly attempt to keep their assets (loans, mortgages) and liabilities (deposits, GICs) matched as to maturity. At these specific maturities, yield spreads between different issuers (Canadas, treasury bills, GICs, strips, and corporates) tend to become compressed. What occurs — and what therefore becomes an opportunity to astute advisors and investors — are yield anomalies. For example, eighteen-month investments typically offer an above-average yield pickup over one-year investments. As a result, those investors willing to stick their necks out for an extra six months will be rewarded when their investment becomes a one-year investment and the yield spreads compress for the reasons advanced above. They may then sell and buy another eighteen-month investment or hold to maturity. Either way, there is a relative yield pickup. A similar anomaly often exists at five years when a one-year extension to six years may offer a higher yield than the slope of the yield curve would suggest. In other words, the investor is rewarded with a higher yield than expected for that extra year. One year hence, the investor will have a five-year investment trading at a far narrower spread than at time of the purchase. As with the one-year/eighteen-month anomaly, the investor may sell and reinvest in another six-year maturity or hold the investment and enjoy the extra yield.

Within the money market itself, the money market yield curve (twelve months and less) offers clues all the time about the near-term direction of short-term interest rates, a subject everyone cares about. The Bank of Canada directly influences short-term interest rates through its actions in the overnight market and the three-month treasury bill market. A little more on the overnight rate: if the Bank of Canada "tightens the system," making it more expensive for jobbers and other market participants to finance their inventories, perhaps to the point where the cost of financing exceeds the yield of the securities, interest rates tend to rise as dealers attempt to shed their inventories since they would lose money by holding them. Everyone attempting this at once is like everyone trying to get out the door at the same time. The Bank of Canada can push rates lower or keep rates low by making it possible to carry inventories at a profit, of course. Past the three-month maturity range, its influence wanes as market forces of supply and demand take over.

The money market yield curve changes frequently. Remembering the general yield curve rules, when short-term money market yields (less than three months) are a lot lower than six- and twelve-month rates (a steep curve), avoid buying the long maturities, since the curve is telling you that short-term rates are too low and/or the cycle for rates is over and rates are headed higher. Frequently, the money market yield curve is flat or inverted. This is a signal to extend term: the cycle is about to turn to lower rates, and the central bank has had to push short-term rates up sharply, typically for currency defence, not for economic reasons. Since the economic fundamentals in such cases argue for lower rates, market participants look past the near term and buy six- or twelve-month bills, knowing that once the currency stabilizes, rates will move lower again and greater returns are to be had in the longer maturities.

Investors who are well-informed can take advantage of certain anomalies that can lead to enhanced returns. These anomalies may occur if there is a very large seller of a bond of a particular maturity or if there is huge demand for another maturity. The net effect is to make a bond of one maturity less or more expensive than would normally be the case. Other factors that can produce such anomalies are a sudden surge in new-issue financings or large purchases by foreign investors. For example, on March 20, 2002, the spread between one-year treasury bills and two-year Canadas was 130 basis points; by September 10, 2002, this spread had narrowed to 15 basis points. These kinds of opportunities occur at various points on the yield curve. They may alert investors that their original selected maturity date turns out to be the "expensive" part of the curve with greater yield available in a neighbouring maturity. Again, investors may return to the original maturity once the anomaly vanishes.

Monetary Policy

It is very important to be aware of monetary policy, as the actions of the Bank of Canada have a bearing on the economy, profits, currency, and the bond market. I will introduce here a simple and practical way to follow monetary policy. Market professionals chart the spread between the two-year Government of Canada benchmark yield and the bank rate as well as the spread between the same two-year bond and the ten-year Canada benchmark. Since the Bank of Canada adopted its regular policy and bank rate setting meetings, the two-year Canada benchmark has become a good proxy for what market participants believe to be the trend in monetary policy. Should the market believe that the Bank of Canada is planning to lower the bank rate and ease monetary policy, it will move the yield on the two-year bond below the bank rate, with the converse being true should the market anticipate a higher bank rate.

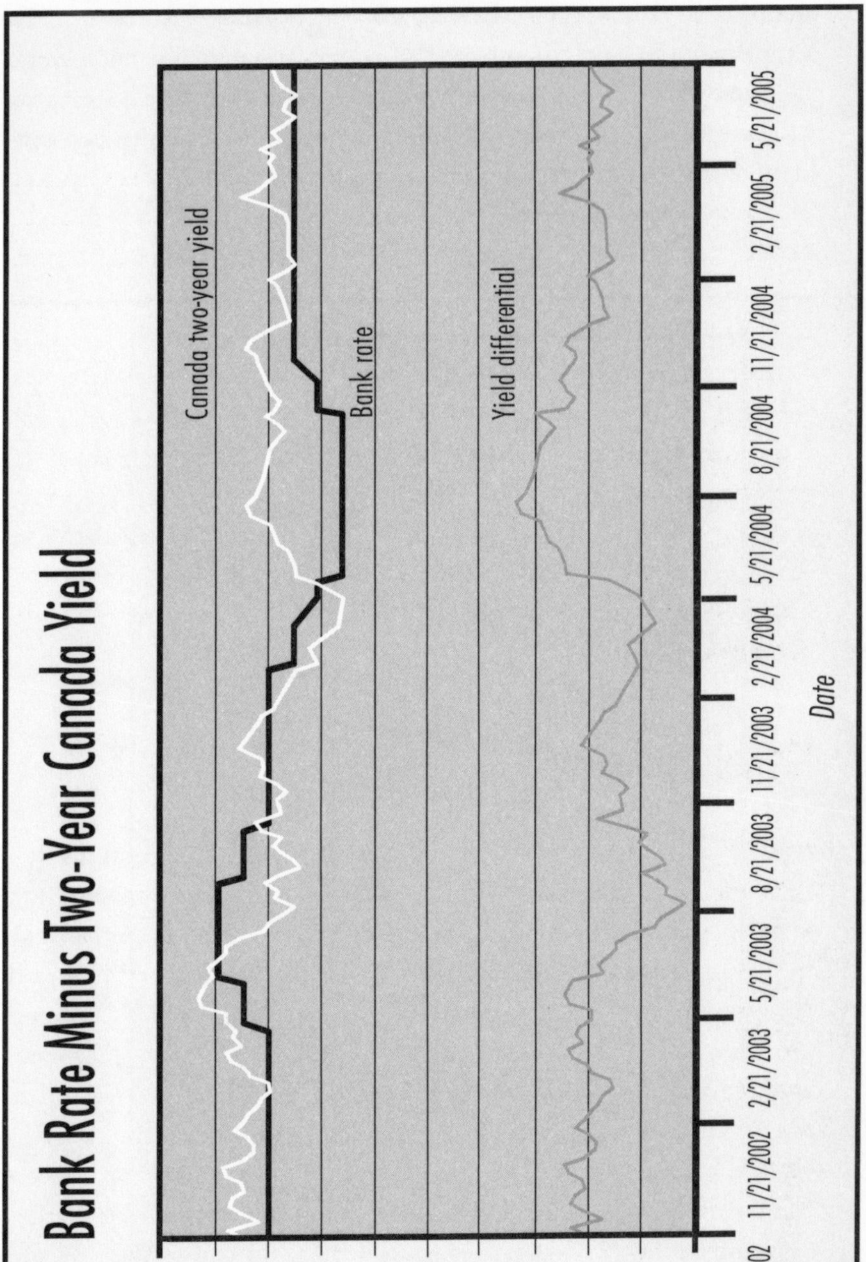
Bank Rate Minus Two-Year Canada Yield
Canada two-year yield
Bank rate
Yield differential
Yield
4
3.5
3
2.5
2
1.5
1
0.5
0
-0.5
-1
8/21/2002
11/21/2002
2/21/2003
5/21/2003
8/21/2003
11/21/2003
2/21/2004
5/21/2004
8/21/2004
11/21/2004
2/21/2005
5/21/2005
Date

The ten-year benchmark trades independently of the bank rate and its yield reflects the collective will of all bond market participants. At a time of extreme monetary ease and an expanding economy, the yield spread from the two-year benchmark to the ten-year benchmark will be very wide (or steep). When monetary policy becomes less stimulating, this spread will narrow, leading to a flattening of the spread. This graph shows the recent trend in this spread:

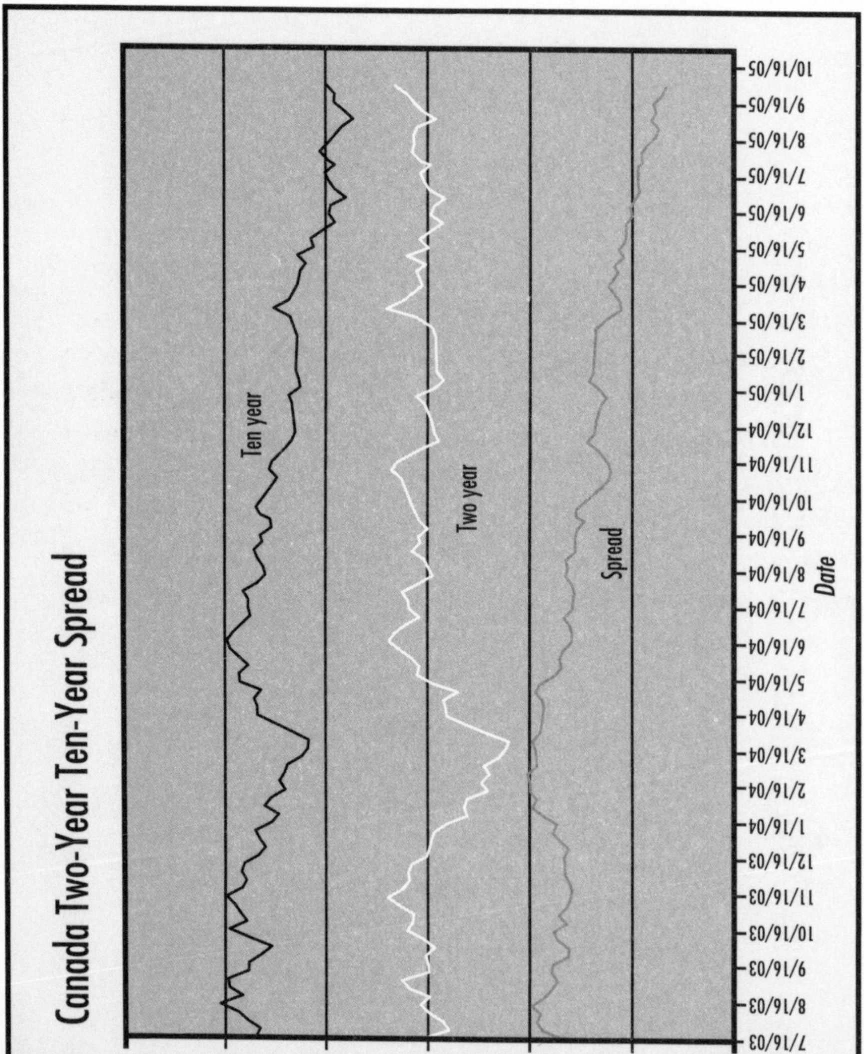

As you can see, this spread peaked at 2 percent and has been steadily falling. It is still a positive spread, indicating that monetary policy is becoming less accommodative but not yet restrictive. You will want to look at both of the above charts at the same time. I recommend charting these spreads weekly, and since you only need three different yields, it should not be overly onerous.

Above all else, make it a point to maintain your own yield curve and keep it current so that you maintain a good perspective on what is happening in the money market and with monetary policy.

So, you made it through the math chapter! The most important point to remember is the present value concept. It shows you that a bond is merely the sum of the present value of all its parts. Now you know something that not more than 5 percent of the investing population knows. Which way do bond prices go when interest rates go up? You know that higher interest rates at different maturities reduce the present value of the parts of a bond and thus the total price or value of the bond moves lower. You also know about duration, which is a vital term as it allows you to judge the relevant volatility or risk of different bonds. (Perhaps go back to the teeter-totter. Someone who is chicken will not sit at the end of the board and thus will have less risk.) You know what basis points are, along with the yield curve, compound interest, and the important topic of reinvestment risk and bond price dynamics.

CHAPTER FOUR
The Products

It is time to discuss the choices facing investors as they seek to assemble their fixed-income portfolios. This is a long chapter, so hang in there. Rule number one: keep it simple. This is sound advice for all investments, not just bonds. If you do not understand a product that is being offered to you, say no!

There are two basic types of issuers of bonds: governments and corporations. The government sector includes the federal government and crown corporations, the provinces, and municipalities. Corporations that issue bonds include industrial, utility, financial, and single-purpose entities. Single purpose entities are one-off companies like GTAA (Greater Toronto Airport Authority). Both of these groups issue different types of products.

Government Securities

Treasury Bills (T-Bills)

These securities are short-term, with a maturity of one year or less (most being issued with terms of three or six months). The federal government also offers one-year bills. At the time of writing, there was $111 billion in Government of Canada T-Bills outstanding. Every second week, the Bank of Canada conducts an auction, inviting the money market jobbers to bid for the amounts being auctioned of three-, six-, and twelve-month maturities. They, in turn, bid for them according to what they consider to be the appropriate yields for the different maturities.

Treasury bills are priced at discounts from their face value. Their yield is the difference between the purchase price and the maturing face or principal amount. The following formula is used when computing the yield of a treasury bill: Y = (100 – P) * 365 / term. (In this formula, *Y* is the quoted yield, *100* is the face value, *P* is the price, and *term* is the number of days remaining to maturity.) Here's an example. A ninety-one-day treasury bill is offered at 99.013. What is the yield? (100-99.013) * 365 / 91 = 4 percent.

You might ask how to compute the price, if you know the yield:

P = 100 / 100 + (Y * term / 365)

Let us then work backwards from the 4 percent yield from the first example:

P =100/100+(4 * 91/365)
= 100/100.99726
= $99.013

You will note that this is not the same as the formula in the present value section. This is because these are short-term, money market securities and the money market functions on an annual yield basis. It is important to grasp the concept of investing in a discounted instrument and receiving your yield when the security matures at a known value in the future. We will return to this concept when we discuss zero coupon bonds, cornerstones of retirement planning. Government of Canada T-Bills are the safest — and the lowest-yielding — money market securities. They are very liquid, with daily trading volumes of $5.6 billion. Investors buy them for safety, to park money for a short term, for market reasons, to keep idle chequing-account deposits earning something, or to put funds aside until they are needed for a specific future event (buying a house, paying taxes, etc.).

Government Bonds

Bonds issued by governments are issued in terms from two years to thirty years and in different currencies. The bulk of these issues are straightforward, paying interest twice a year with no special features, so investors are attracted to them for their safety, yield, lack of complication, variety of maturities, and liquidity. All governments have taxing power; in fact, we taxpayers all provide the security for these bonds. It has been refreshing these past five years to see the end of deficit financing and some paying down of our national debt. It creates a virtuous circle where some of the surplus is applied to reducing debt, resulting in lower debt payments, which leads to a bigger surplus to pay down more debt. This shows no sign of ending in Canada soon, although the big spenders are eyeing our money anxiously.

This positive development has caused some change in the way the bond market functions. For example, even though the federal government is paying down debt, it still recognizes the importance of having liquid benchmark issues so that market participants can hedge their inventories and also provide reference points for new issue pricing. The Bank of Canada has been conducting a program of buying in older, smaller, less-liquid Government of Canada issues and replacing them with additions to the benchmark issues at the important maturity dates: two, three, five, ten, and thirty years. These become very large issues and are the most liquid in the marketplace. As the government debt shrinks, the Bank of Canada (as agent for the government) is committed to maintaining large benchmark issues. These issues also allow investment dealers to hedge their inventories by shorting the benchmarks against all their long positions or to hedge a new issue that is selling slowly. Swap desks, which are involved in the business of swapping fixed rate liabilities for floating rate ones, among other things, are frequently large buyers or sellers of these high-quality, fixed-rate benchmarks. In addition, when IAs or the media need to know what is happening in the bond market, they will refer to one or more of these issues, sometimes using the term *bellwether*, as in "The bellwether 5 3/4s of 2029 are up 50 cents in active trading."

Of course, they also provide the foundation for the yield curve, which, as we have seen, can be an important analytical tool. And as you will see in the zero coupon section, they are the base for the bond stripping business. They provide easy entry and exit from the bond market for those money managers who attempt to guess which way bond prices are going, for foreign investors, and for individual speculators.

Provincial Bonds

Provincial bonds are similar to the federal ones but offer slightly higher yields as their governments' taxing power is confined to the individual provinces. Here is where the various provinces trade on a yield spread basis from the Canada benchmarks:

Provincial Yield Spreads from Canadas (July 2005)

	5 years	10 years	30 years
Ontario	26.2	39.8	62.5
Br. Columbia	24.8	34.5	51.5
Alberta	14.6	36.5	n/a
Manitoba	24.5	39.2	55.0
Saskatchewan	24.8	38.7	56.8
Quebec	34.0	57.2	76.6
Nova Scotia	28.6	42.5	67.7
New Brunswick	25.1	42.4	66.5
Newfoundland	32.0	42.5	73.2
Pr. Edward Island	38.6	56.5	71.1

These yield spreads are relatively modest and closely bunched. This is owing to the improved fiscal condition of all the provinces. Alberta may be totally debt-free in a few years. This has not always been the case, as the ebb and flow of the political events in Quebec has produced some startling swings. Also, these days provincial issuers are adding to existing issues regularly, augmenting their liquidity and popularity. Thus, investors can pick up some extra yield in safe, liquid provincial bonds.

Municipal Bonds

Municipalities also borrow money for capital purposes. There was a time when each town or city would issue its own bonds. Those days are mostly gone. Most provinces have created municipal borrowing authorities (Alberta Municipal Finance Corp. and New Brunswick Municipal Finance Corp. are examples) that use their lower interest costs to borrow money on behalf of the various municipalities. The bonds that they issue are guarantees of the provinces and therefore trade at the same yield as straight provincial debt. There are a few exceptions, naturally. Ontario has created regional governments, such as the Regional Municipality of Ottawa-Carleton, which assume borrowing power for all the towns and villages in their areas. Also, Canada's largest cities, such as Montreal, Toronto, and Vancouver, still issue bonds in their own names. Unlike in the United States, there are no tax advantages to owning municipal bonds in Canada.

Structured Notes

Crown corporations, provinces, and banks issue structured notes aimed primarily at the individual investor. While not necessarily in your best interest, you will need to know about them. Let's discuss step-ups. Step-up bonds are issued mostly by provinces, crown corporations, and banks. They are not straightforward. They are called step-ups because they have several potential maturity dates. Interest is paid at a certain rate to a certain date and then the interest rate "steps up" to a higher rate and so on. They offer an attractive yield spread over the corresponding maturity dates of conventional bonds. What is the catch? They are callable by the issuer at each date. This means that the issuer or borrower may return your money to you at any of the callable dates so there is a lot of uncertainty about the life of your investment. Also, if the issuer does not call the bond, it is usually because rates have risen and the yield you are receiving is below where new step-ups or conventional bonds are being offered and so the value of your investment goes down. Here is an example of a step-up issued by the Province of Manitoba:

Province of Manitoba
Issue Size: $10,000,000
Initial Maturity Date: July 31, 2006
Final Maturity Date: July 31, 2017

Step-up Coupon Rates:

July 31, 2005 to July 31, 2006	4.00%
July 31 ,2006 to July 31, 2007	4.10%
July 31, 2007 to July 31, 2008	4.20%
July 31, 2008 to July 31, 2009	4.30%
July 31 ,2009 to July 31, 2010	4.40%
July 31, 2010 to July 31, 2011	4.50%
July 31, 2011 to July 31, 2012	4.60%
July 31, 2012 to July 31, 2013	4.70%
July 31, 2013 to July 31, 2014	4.80%
July 31, 2014 to July 31, 2015	5.00%
July 31, 2015 to July 31, 2016	5.20%
July 31, 2016 to July 31, 2017	5.40%

The issuer, Manitoba, may extend the bond, *at its option*, on each payment date. Thus, the investor will not know how long the investment will last. If interest rates move lower, Manitoba would likely not extend this bond, but would refinance it at lower yield. If rates rise, then it would likely extend it. The yield to the initial maturity date of July 31,2006, of 4 percent was 99 basis points higher than one-year government treasury bills. If this issue were extended to its final maturity date, the yield to maturity of 4.54 percent would be 53 basis points higher than the Government of Canada curve. If interest rates continued to fall the Province of Manitoba would choose not to extend the maturity date. Meanwhile, the investors in these bonds, salivating over those bigger coupon payments in the subsequent maturity dates, would suddenly find themselves scrambling to lend money at lower rates while the Province of Manitoba calmly issued bonds at lower rates. This underscores the fact the features on these step-up bonds are all in the hands of the issuers.

They can be attractive investments at certain times but should be avoided when interest rates are rising, or when the yield curve is becoming flatter.

Zero Coupon Bonds

Imagine an investment that is high quality, liquid, and fully compounding, with a future value that is known to the exact penny. This is the zero coupon bond. The zero coupon bond has become the cornerstone of the fixed-income portion of RRSPs. As the baby boomers work their way towards retirement, they are looking for more certainty, and zero coupons offer them just that. A detailed description of these bonds follows in the next chapter. Given a certain amount to invest today, you can buy a zero coupon of a specific maturity and you will know exactly what you will receive at that maturity date. As well, these are almost all government bonds and are very safe.

They are created by traders for investment dealers who purchase a block of bonds and then separate or "strip" the individual interest and principal payments from each other, applying a discount yield to these payments to compute a present value (remember the present value calculation from Chapter 3). This present value becomes the cost, and this strip will then compound at the purchase yield to the future payment amount. There are no payments received during that time, which is where the name *zero coupon* comes from.

This is a terrific retirement product. The market for strips is huge, with $185 billion of face value outstanding and trading volume of $9.5 billion per month.

Retirement Savings Bonds (RSBs)

Suppose you have ten years to retirement, at which time you will need regular income. Is there a product that can accomplish this feat? Yes! The RSB is a partially stripped bond. The coupon payments for the years for which you do not need income are stripped from the bond, with the rest of the bond being left intact. When the ten-year period, in this example, is up, interest payments begin, producing a regular stream of income. These RSBs are sold at a discount reflecting the present value of the deferred income stream. In fact, they are deferred annuities that offer attractive yields and liquidity as well. They already exist in many forms, trade in the secondary market, and can be created easily to custom specifications by your friendly stripper.

Inflation and Real Return Bonds

Inflation is the enemy of bonds. At an inflation rate of approximately 5 percent, a dollar's purchasing power shrinks to just 61 cents in only ten years! Since most fixed-income instruments pay a fixed rate of interest, inflation will erode the purchasing power of those payments over time. Investors, cognizant of this fact, expect to earn a real return (yield minus inflation) of 2 percent before taxes on government bonds. The question then becomes which inflation rate to use to compute a real return: the past twelve months, the average for the past five years, or the inflation expectations for the next one or several years? It appears that the expected future rate of inflation is the key variable.

The fact that inflation is so unpredictable helps to explain why I am a strong advocate of laddered portfolios. With a steady progression of maturing bonds, an investor will have money available at different times to reinvest at prevailing interest rates, which, of course, will reflect the inflation expectations at that moment. Should interest rates spike higher, then maturing funds would be available to reinvest at higher yields. The converse is true, of course, should interest rates move lower, but over the course of a couple of economic cycles, investors would find the laddered approach to be in their best interest as they spread their investments over the cycles. Furthermore, it eliminates the risk of having all of their fixed-income investments maturing at the low point of the interest rate cycle, which would almost guarantee poor real returns, as inflation and interest rates would then move higher through the economic cycle.

While the laddered approach is my preferred method of ensuring positive real returns, there is another fixed-income instrument available that guarantees real returns and also serves as a useful proxy for inflation expectations. This is the real return bond (RRB). In Canada, RRBs are issued primarily by the Government of Canada, and they protect the future purchasing power not only of the principal but also of the interest payments. For a comprehensive analysis of these complex securities, I recommend visiting the Bank of Canada's website (www.bankofcanada.ca). While these are complex securities, there is a healthy market for them. At the time of writing, there are four issues outstanding, totalling $19.4 billion. The issues are the 4.25 percent due December 1, 2021, the 4.25 percent due December 1, 2026, the 4 percent due December 1, 2031, and the 3 percent due December 1, 2036. Note that they are issued with a nominal coupon rate. Thus, as inflationary expectations wax and wane, the price of these bonds will rise and fall accordingly.

Who buys them? Pension funds, particularly non-profit ones such as municipal or provincial plans, are the most common buyers, as RRBs are very useful for meeting or exceeding actuarial assumptions. Their complexity makes these bonds unfriendly to individual investors. While not as liquid as other Canada bonds, there is a decent market for them nonetheless. The real problem is that IAs will not see any repeat business since RRBs are primarily buy-and-hold investments. This is not to say that they do not have significant price swings. Their price fluctuations arise from shifting inflation expectations. Following is a chart showing the changing yield over time:

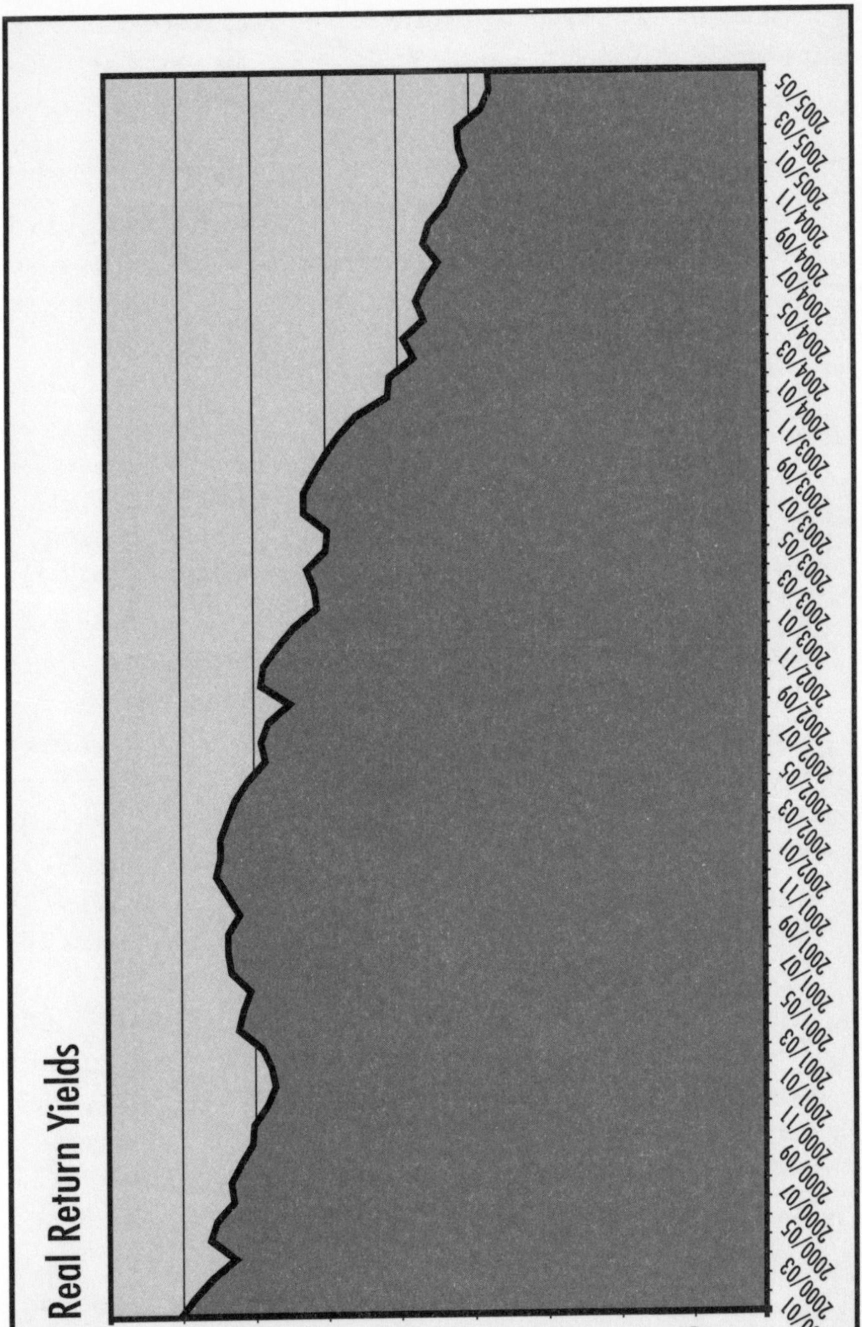

Real Return Yields
4.5
4
3.5
3
2.5
2
1.5
1
0.5
0
2000/01
2000/03
2000/05
2000/07
2000/09
2000/11
2001/01
2001/03
2001/05
2001/07
2001/09
2001/11
2002/01
2002/03
2002/05
2002/07
2002/09
2002/11
2003/01
2003/03
2003/05
2003/07
2003/09
2003/11
2004/01
2004/03
2004/05
2004/07
2004/09
2004/11
2005/01
2005/03
2005/05

To underscore what this fall in yields has done to the price of a real return bond, here is a chart of the Canada 4 percent due December 1, 2031:

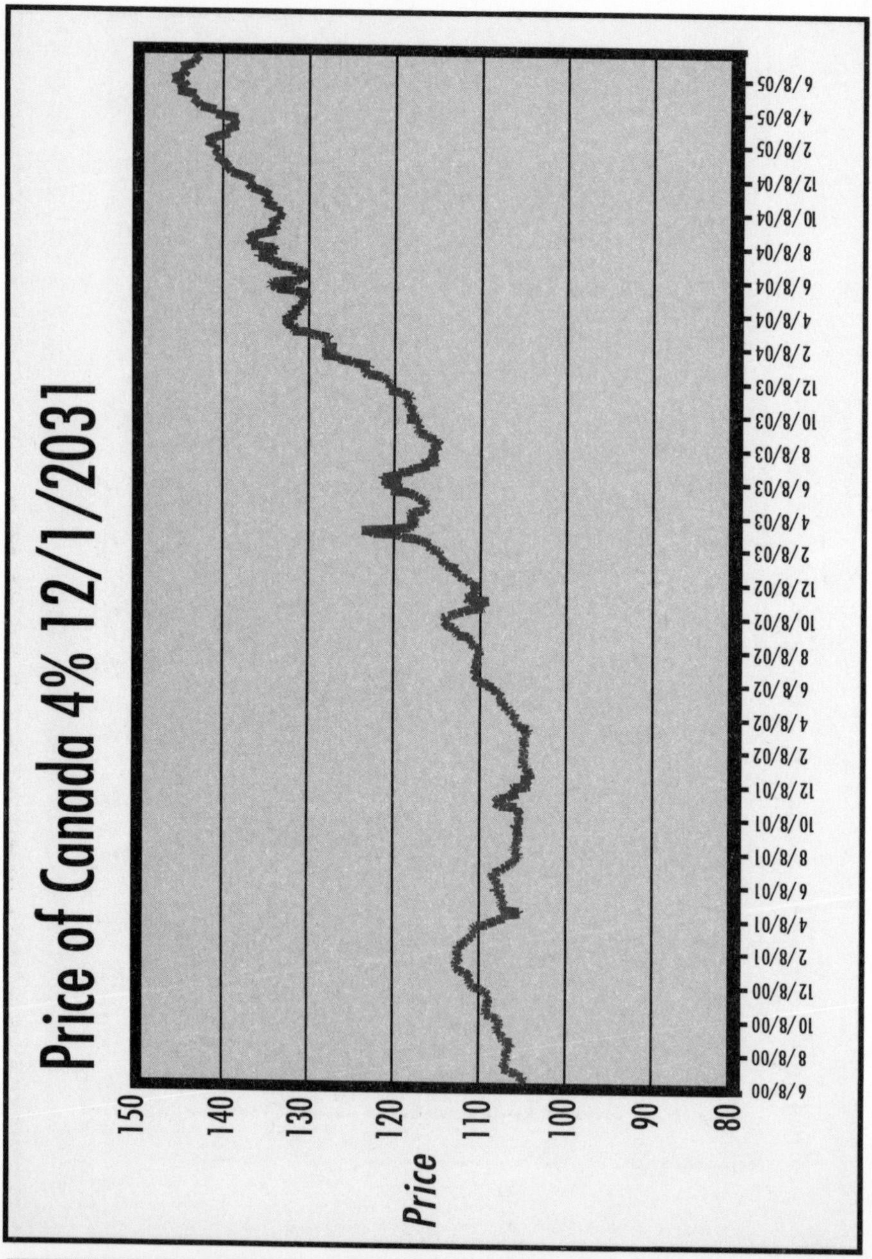

As well, it is useful to compare the yield on RRBs to that of conventional Canada bonds in order to further gauge market expectations.

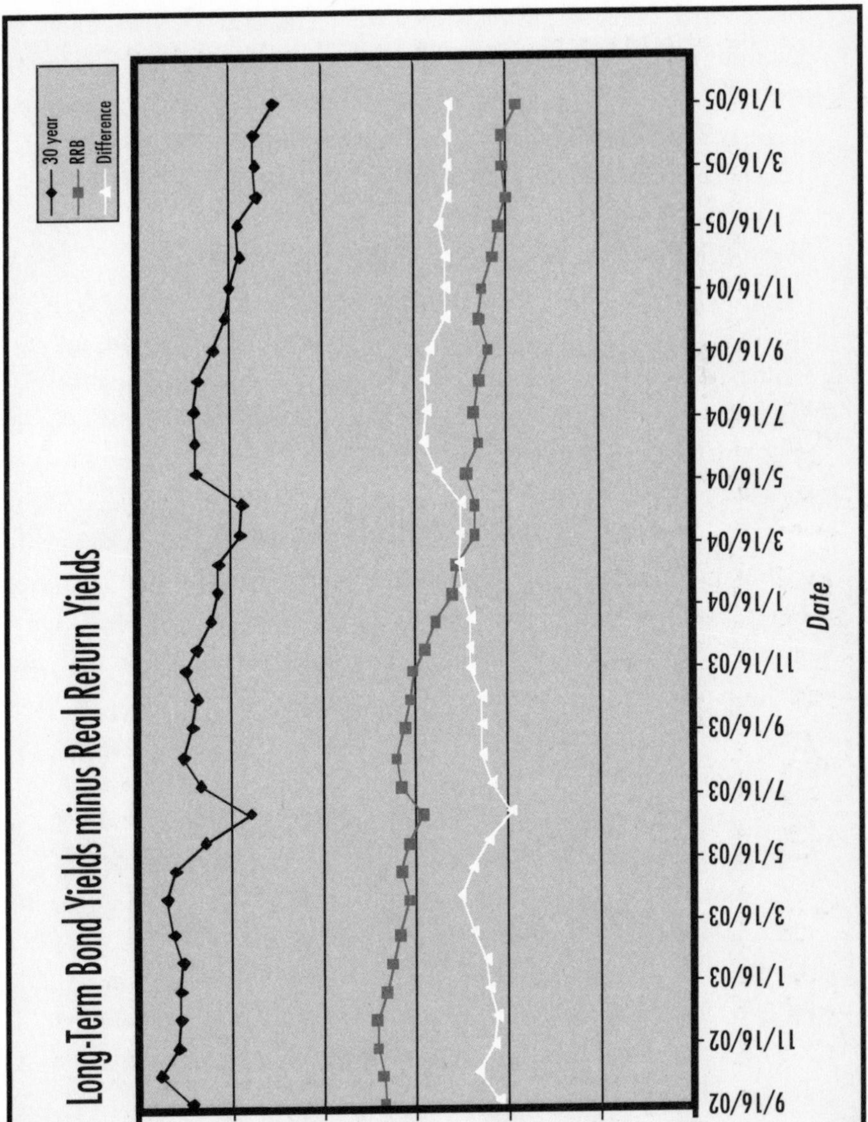

As RRBs are often too complex for individual investors, the laddered approach is a far simpler and more effective way to protect yourselves from inflation. One useful approach to take with the RRBs is to calculate the break-even inflation rate. This is the inflation rate at which the total return on nominal bonds and real return bonds is equal. At present, this rate is 1.9 percent, down from 2.6 percent in 2003. With inflation and inflation expectations falling, this does not appear to be a good time to buy RRBs. This is because the real yield would have to rise so that the break-even yield was equal to the Consumer Price Index. Therefore, their price would have to fall for the real yield to rise.

Mortgage-backed Securities

Since the early 1990s, financial institutions have been selling off large parts of their mortgage portfolios by packaging them up and selling them as securities called mortgage-backed securities (MBS). MBS are not technically government securities, but because they offer the National Housing Act guarantee plus a first mortgage on the properties themselves, they are very high quality and are considered semi-government securities. As well, they offer a blended monthly payment of principal and interest. Of course, they are the flip side of a mortgage. As anyone who has bought a house and financed via a mortgage knows, monthly payments consist of both principal and interest. With MBS, investors are receiving a blended payment, and yet when they sell them, many of them complain because their principal amount has shrunk!

In an MBS pool, the various payments are recorded, and what is called a "pool factor" is calculated, indicating what percentage of the original principal remains. There are different kinds of MBS pools, the most common being non-prepayable (where the borrowers may not pay down their principal early) and prepayable (where they may). The prepayable pools have greater volatility since the borrowers can pay off their principal in lump sums. The non-prepayables thus offer a more predictable cash flow.

I am always astonished when I hear IAs complain that their clients' original face value has shrunk by a significant amount. They just don't get this principal repayment idea.

The appeal of MBS, besides their quality, is the monthly income. Given the problems that that IAs and clients have with the principal payment issue, the investment bankers have managed to get a few borrowers to issue monthly pay bonds where the monthly payment is only interest. There are several issuers, so ask your IA for a list. Should these issues not be available, it is possible for your IA to construct portfolios where the interest payment dates are staggered to produce monthly payments. Sometimes they can even be laddered! But overall, MBS are usually too complicated for individual investors. My advice, if you need monthly income, is to buy monthly pay bonds that pay just interest monthly or to construct a portfolio whose interest payments fall in such a way that you receive a cheque each month.

U.S. Bonds

The American bond market is the biggest and most liquid bond market in the world. Canadian investors sometimes need to buy U.S.–dollar securities. This could be because they intend to retire in the United States and would therefore need U.S.–dollar income, because they have a negative view of the Canadian currency, or because interest rates are higher there.

The American market, of course, offers a broad and diverse product list. The market is divided into three separate categories: the domestic market (for U.S. government, agency bonds, stripped bonds, and domestic corporate bonds); the Yankee market (which refers to U.S–dollar bonds issued by Canadian borrowers); and the municipal tax-exempt market (which has no appeal for Canadian investors as they trade on an after-tax basis).

With respect to American government and corporate issues, there may be tax considerations that may make them unattractive to a Canadian investor. Nevertheless, the American government bond market offers immense liquidity and very narrow bid-ask spreads. In Canada, the bid-ask spread is typically five to ten cents on benchmark Canadas, whereas in the United States, it is one sixty-fourth (.015625) of a cent on a U.S. government bond! Active traders and speculators are assured of liquidity and tight pricing, even for small quantities. The American market also offers U.S. government strips and real return bonds (called TIPS). U.S. government bonds and domestic corporates are foreign content for Canadian investors but are now fully eligible after the removal of foreign content restrictions for Canadians in the 2005 federal budget. As the most liquid Government of Canada benchmarks are considered the bellwethers in the Canadian bond market, U.S. benchmark bonds are the bellwethers for the entire global bond market. The U.S. ten-year benchmark issue (currently the 4.125 percent due May 15, 2015) is the most closely watched individual bond in the world. Therefore, it would be in your best interest to start following it from the daily newspapers, online from sites such as Bloomberg.com, or from your IA's firm. If your IA's FI has it on its website, make a point of tracking it. While you may not be considering investing in U.S. government bonds, this particular bond and its yield affect a lot of other bond and equity markets, so a big change in the price of it could affect your investment decision in any number of investment categories. Perhaps a surprise uptick in the rate of inflation might cause a sudden sharp decline in the price of the U.S. ten-year benchmark (and a corresponding rise in its yield). A lot of these sharp swings prove to be temporary or are overdone, thus presenting you with an investment opportunity or window to take advantage of. The Canadian bond market is tightly correlated with the American bond market, so it pays to be aware of what is happening there. There is a steady parade of economic statistics in both the United States and Canada, which can move markets. Learn about these from your IA and ask for the calendar of upcoming releases or look for them in publications such as *Barrons* or the *Financial Post*. They come out at specific times of the day and some are more important than others.

Thus, the American bond market is important to you even if you are not contemplating an investment in it. Later, in the technical section, we cover how to chart bonds. The U.S. ten-year benchmark would be the first to chart.

Should you have needs for U.S.–dollar fixed-income investments, you might also consider Yankee bonds. A Yankee bond is one issued by a Canadian borrower in U.S. dollars.

The Yankee market is an attractive alternative for Canadian investors. For example, the Province of Ontario may choose to issue bonds denominated in U.S. dollars. Even though the principal and interest are payable in U.S. dollars, these bonds are *not* considered foreign content, since they were issued by a Canadian entity, nor do they have any adverse tax implications. (Of course, following the 2005 budget, foreign content is no longer an issue for Canadian investors.)

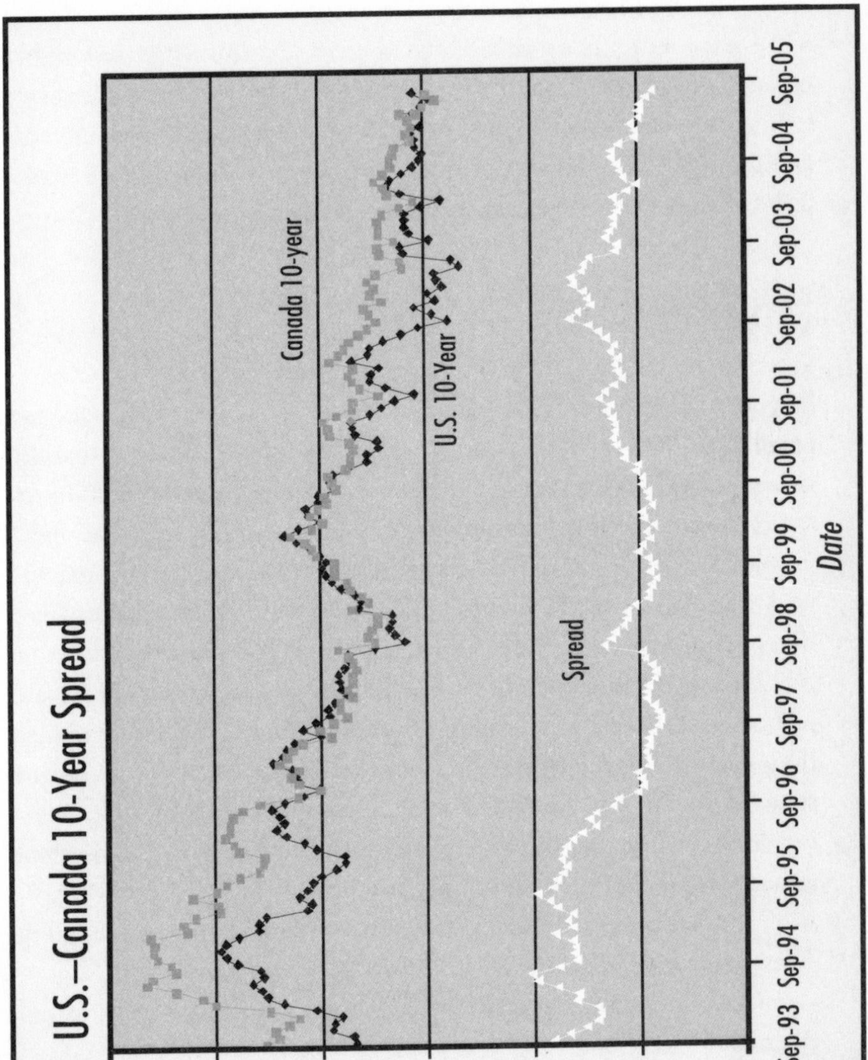

The major Canadian investment dealers have American subsidiaries that make markets in all of the American pay bonds, making it relatively easy to obtain bids and offerings. American yields are almost always lower than Canadian yields, although that has not been the case for the past year and a half as a result of our strong currency and the triple surpluses (budgetary, trade, and current account). The spread among the various maturities expands and contracts, offering some excellent opportunities for traders and investors alike. For example, from the perspective of a Canadian investor looking to buy U.S. government bonds, the spread at the ten-year maturity for government bonds since 1999 has ranged from a positive spread of 45 basis points to a negative spread of 122 basis points.

Corporate Bonds

It is in your best interest to learn as much about corporate bonds as possible for two essential reasons: one, they offer more yield than do government bonds; and two, unlike governments, some corporations go out of business, so investors must pay close attention to credit ratings.

First, let us review what a bond is. When we discuss the bond market, we are referring, in a broad sense, to all the fixed-income instruments that trade. In the narrow definition, a bond refers to an obligation that is backed by specific assets. These could include factories, rail cars, airplanes, or credit card receivables. Investors would have first claim on these assets in case of default. Let's use the first mortgage on a house as an example. A financial institution lends you money to help buy a property, but in return, it has a first mortgage or claim on it if, for some reason, you default on your payments.

So, what are bonds called that are not backed by specific assets? They are called debentures. Technically, what the Government of Canada and the provinces issue are debentures, but in practice, we call their issues bonds.

Practically all the corporate bonds issued these days are also debentures, so debenture holders have an unsecured claim on corporate assets. Governments issue bonds to cover a deficit or to refinance a maturing issue. Corporations have more specific reasons for issuing debentures, such as building factories or pipelines. Sometimes, they are paying off bank debt incurred when building those assets. A bond issue can be tailored to the life expectancy of an asset.

There is a wide array of corporations, but we will try to break them down into a few categories: utilities, industrials, financials, and single-purpose entities. To facilitate assessing the creditworthiness of corporations, there are several agencies that produce credit ratings on all the debt, both short-term and long-term, issued by companies (for example, Moody's, Standard and Poor, and Dominion Bond Rating Service). They assign a credit rating for each debt layer of a company and are constantly reviewing them, issuing upgrades and downgrades when necessary.

One critical level for corporate credit ratings is the investment grade level. BBB is the lowest level at which many institutions may invest in corporate bonds. Below that level — BB (High) or less — bonds enter what is called the high-yield bond or junk-bond levels, where fewer lenders venture and where financing becomes more difficult. Credit ratings begin at AAA (or "triple A") for the best borrowers and descend from there. Each level has three tiers, for example AAA (High), AAA (Mid), and AAA (Low). Then there are AA, then A, and then BBB, with each level having the same three tiers. These ratings are not foolproof, but they provide a very useful reference point for investors. In addition, the major investment dealers all offer comprehensive research on companies. While a great percentage of it is aimed at the equity value of a company, there is specific research available regarding the debt quality of corporations, investment grade and not. Corporate bond offerings are normally accompanied by the credit rating. If not, ask for it. You should also check to see if the rating has changed recently or whether it is under review.

Corporate bonds frequently have elements not typically found on other bonds. Government bonds typically pay interest semi-annually and pay the principal at maturity. While there are some similar corporates, they normally have additional features.

The most common one is a callable feature, meaning that the corporation, under certain conditions, may call the debentures back from the investors. Why would a company call its bonds back? It could be because it has enough cash and wishes to reduce its indebtedness, or a corporate event such as a merger or takeover might have occurred. What would such a feature look like? Here is a specific example: in 2003 Bell Canada issued $600 million 5.5 percent due August 12, 2010 bonds at $99.678, to yield 5.55 percent, 70 basis points above the Canada yield curve. The call feature states that this company may call, or redeem, this issue, but only at the greater price of $100 or 17.5 basis points above the Canada yield curve, whichever price is higher. In this case, even though investors may lose their investment, it is on relatively attractive terms — 52.5 basis points better than when it was issued. If this bond had been called the day after it was issued, BCE would have had to pay bondholders $102.94 to yield 5.025 percent.

Overall, call features are not in your best interest, as your investment may be called from you when you did not want your money back. The option to call is in the issuers' hands.

Money Market Instruments

Banks issue bankers' acceptances (BAs), which are corporate promissory notes stamped by the banks as guaranteed. They typically yield more than treasury bills but less than commercial paper and are also very liquid. Like T-Bills, they trade at a discount from face value.

Corporations issue commercial paper, which is merely an unsecured promissory note to repay; commercial paper is riskier and yields more than treasury bills.

Money market securities thus offer safety and income for those investors with short-term needs.

High-Yield or Junk Bonds

With nominal interest rates so low these days (even though real yields are about where they normally are), many investors are tempted to reach for the very high yields offered by corporate bonds issued by companies whose credit ratings have fallen below the investment-grade levels. When that happens, many investing institutions can no longer buy them and, in fact, some may have to sell them. What typically happens is that the price of the bonds falls precipitously, offering what appear to be very high yields. The bid/ask on these types of bonds becomes very wide ($3 to $5), with poor liquidity and sudden, large price swings. Your IAs may offer certain of these bonds to you. Many of these situations have worked out (Telus, Stelco, Nortel, Hudson's Bay, and others), but there have been some spectacular flameouts (Air Canada). I recommend the following approach to these "fallen angels":

Diversify your risk. If you wish to invest in them yourself, buy several different issues.

Shop around. Prices may vary widely from one FI to another, and IAs like to charge higher-than-average markups on these bonds.

Do your homework. With the high-yield bonds, it is important to understand the value of the company and what the equity is worth. Obtain equity research on the individual companies and ask your IAs for debt research, too. The major FIs all have fixed income research on corporate bonds.

Consider high-yield mutual funds. These are the only mutual funds I would ever suggest. The yields are high enough to justify the MERs, and you will actually receive professional management!

So, how do you go about investing in corporate bonds? Very carefully. But with due diligence and a knowledgeable IA with a good firm, you can start to earn some incremental yield. Most new corporate issues are sold only to institutional investors because it is economical for the underwriters to do so. It is all about money. Most IAs get a 50 percent payout on commissions, whereas institutional groups are paid a lot less, so it behooves a major dealer to sell as little as possible to the retail investor.

There are some issuers who insist that some of their issues be distributed to retail customers and a few who do specific retail-targeted deals, but they are the exception. Therefore, most of your retail corporate bond investing will be done in the secondary market and with certain mid-term note (MTN) issuers. MTN issuers file what is called a shelf prospectus, which permits them, on short notice, to bring a bond issue to market without the need for a full prospectus. This process allows them to take advantage of a sudden drop in yields or perhaps to fill a void in the market when there is not much supply and lots of demand. Regular borrowers such as car companies and utilities are the largest issuers of MTNs.

How do you proceed? Let us examine the laddered approach. In the corporate bond world, you not only want different maturity dates but different issuers as well, to spread out your credit risk. Needing income but not much risk, investors may put together a ladder of the higher-rated corporates (household names such as the big banks, Bell Canada, etc.), which will produce higher yields than would a ladder of government bonds. There will be moments when investors are tempted to invest in something that appears to offer an exceptional yield when compared to other corporate bonds. There is usually a good reason why something appears to be cheap, so it is in your best interest to dig deep to learn more. There could be a punitive call feature, or the company in question may be facing a downgrade to less-than-investment-grade status.

Fixed/Floaters

Typically issued by the banks, these bonds look like this: Royal Bank 6.75 percent June 4, 2012/2007. To qualify as Tier 1 capital, these bonds were issued with a ten-year maturity but only paying a fixed rate of interest for five years, after which they "float" at three-month bankers' acceptances plus 100 basis points if the bank does not call them. In practice, these bonds are called at the end of the fixed period, as there is no reason for a bank to pay 1 percent over BAs. This is because BAs trade at small yield spreads over treasury bills and banks can borrow money very cheaply. This is an artificial floating rate, and the bonds are valued to the end of the fixed-rate period.

Asset-backed Securities

These bonds are typically created by a company such as Canadian Tire, which has credit card receivables. It packages them together and issues a bond using the receivables as collateral. In other words, the credit card payments flow through to the bond holders. In order to ensure that the bonds are adequately backed, issuers typically over-collateralize the bonds, perhaps to the tune of 125 percent of the size of the bond issue. This takes care of any possible shortfalls from delinquent or defaulted payments.

Convertible Bonds

There also exist bonds that offer investors both interest income and an option to convert into the underlying common equity of a corporation. The combination of income and potential growth is attractive to investors. These hybrid securities are issued by corporations and carry similar features to conventional bonds, in that they offer a fixed coupon rate (normally paid semi-annually) and have a specific maturity date. They differ from conventional bonds in two distinct ways. First, they offer investors a feature where the investors may "convert" their bonds into the underlying common equity of the issuing company. There is usually a specific conversion price at which investors may convert. Second, they rank junior to other indebtedness of the issuing company and therefore have more credit risk. Terms on convertible bonds vary from issue to issue, so careful analysis is required.

Here is an example of a convertible bond: Hudson's Bay Company 7.5 percent due December 1, 2008. Conversion terms: convertible into 57.5374 shares of Hudson's Bay Company per $1,000 face value. This equates to a conversion price of $1,000/57.5374, or $17.38 per Hudson's Bay share.

These bonds may be called in two different ways by the company: anytime the common shares trade at or above $21.725 for twenty consecutive business days out of thirty consecutive business days, or on thirty days' notice at par after December 2, 2006.

At the time of writing, these bonds were trading at $103.80 and the common shares of Hudson's Bay were at $14.25. Since each bond is convertible into 57.5374 shares, the intrinsic value is $14.25 * 57.5373, or $819.90. However, the market value of one debenture is $1,038, so we call the difference ($1,038 - $819.90, or $218.10) the conversion premium. Hudson's Bay pays a dividend on its common shares of 36 cents per share, producing a dividend yield of 2.52 percent. The debentures at $103.80 have a current yield of 7.22 percent. Thus, the debentures pay more in income than do the common shares by 4.70 percent per annum, which is not enough of an excess to pay off the premium of 26.6 percent ($218.10 / $819.90) by maturity. In this case, investors would be better off buying the common shares. You might wonder what happens if the price of the common equity does not rise above the conversion price. Well, for one thing you do not convert, and since these bonds have a maturity date, you will receive your principal back at maturity, having collected the accrued interest along the way.

Many companies that issue convertibles do not pay dividends, so in those cases, convertible bonds usually make more sense. Overall, convertible debentures can be attractive investments offering both income and growth potential. However, investors must arm themselves with research as to the merits of the underlying equity of the company in question before considering investing in them.

Corporate bonds are normally the highest yielding ones in the bond market, and so they attract a lot of investor attention. At the same time, there are unique aspects to every issue, requiring investors to be sure what it is they are buying. As always, simpler is better, so look for straightforward, uncomplicated corporate bonds with credit ratings of BBB or better. Make sure you obtain all the relevant information for any corporate bond that interests you.

CHAPTER FIVE
Zero Coupon Bonds

The next two chapters deal with the two most important aspects of fixed-income investing for individual investors: zero coupon bonds and the laddered approach to portfolio construction. Combining these simple but very effective products and strategies will add yield to your portfolios and enhance your retirement nest egg.

Known commonly as "stripped bonds," "strips," or "zeros," zero coupon bonds (so called because they are bonds that pay no interest) have become cornerstones for retirement planning. I will use the term *strips* to describe them henceforth. Strips are also called coupons, residuals, Tigrs, Sentinels, and Cougars. They are created by treating each interest payment on a bond as a separate security or obligation to pay a certain finite amount at a specified future date. What follows is an example of the cash flow of an actual bond, the one that we have been using throughout the book as an example, the Canada 5 percent due June 1, 2014. We will assume a face value of $100,000, a market price of $107.15, and a yield to maturity of 4 percent (as of December 1, 2005). The total cost would equal $107,150 (100,000 * 1.0715) since there is no accrued interest to pay. December 1 is an interest payment date, so it makes all of these examples easier to understand.

Almost all domestic bonds pay interest twice a year, so each payment equals $2,500 ($100,000 * .05 / 2).

Components of an Actual Bond

	Interest	Face Value
June 1, 2006	$ 2,500	
December 1, 2006	$ 2,500	
June 1, 2007	$ 2,500	
December 1, 2007	$ 2,500	
June 1, 2008	$ 2,500	
December 1, 2008	$ 2,500	
June 1, 2009	$ 2,500	
December 1, 2009	$ 2,500	
June 1, 2010	$ 2,500	
December 1, 2010	$ 2,500	
June 1, 2011	$ 2,500	
December 1, 2011	$ 2,500	
June1, 2012	$ 2,500	
December 1, 2012	$ 2,500	
June 1, 2013	$ 2,500	
December 1, 2013	$ 2,500	
June 1, 2014	$ 2,500	
June 1, 2014		$100,000
	$42,500	

As you can plainly see, this bond has eighteen components, seventeen interest payments, and one principal payment — the repayment of the initial loan. Since each of these payments is a separate obligation of the borrower, there is no reason they cannot be separated from each other and then treated as individual securities. In fact, evaluating the present value of each of these parts allows us to calculate the value of the bond.

Present Value of Bond Parts

Date	Interest Payment	Par Value	Discount Rate	Present Value of $1	Value
June 1, 2006	$2,500		4.00%	0.98039	$ 2,450.98
December 1, 2006	$2,500		4.00%	0.96117	$ 2,402.93
June 1, 2007	$2,500		4.00%	0.94232	$ 2,355.80
December 1, 2007	$2,500		4.00%	0.92385	$ 2,309.63
June 1, 2008	$2,500		4.00%	0.90573	$ 2,264.33
December 1, 2008	$2,500		4.00%	0.88797	$ 2,219.93
June 1, 2009	$2,500		4.00%	0.87056	$ 2,176.40
December 1, 2009	$2,500		4.00%	0.85349	$ 2,133.73
June 1, 2010	$2,500		4.00%	0.83676	$ 2,091.90
December 1, 2010	$2,500		4.00%	0.82035	$ 2,050.88
June 1, 2011	$2,500		4.00%	0.80426	$ 2,010.65
December 1, 2011	$2,500		4.00%	0.78849	$ 1,971.23
June 1, 2012	$2,500		4.00%	0.77303	$ 1,932.58
December 1, 2012	$2,500		4.00%	0.75788	$ 1,894.70
June 1, 2013	$2,500		4.00%	0.74301	$ 1,857.53
December 1, 2013	$2,500		4.00%	0.72845	$ 1,821.13
June 1, 2014	$2,500		4.00%	0.71416	$ 1,785.40
June 1, 2014		$100,000	4.00%	0.71416	$71,416.00
Total	$ 42,500				
Grand Total	**$142,500**				**$107,145.68**

You will notice that by calculating the present value of each component of the bond at the purchase yield, we arrive at the exact cost of the bond as seen above: $107.15. Thus, a bond is again demonstrated to be the sum of its parts.

We have now made each of these payments into a separate security and can offer them as discount securities, which compound at a given yield to a precise future value. Think of them as long-term treasury bills where the yield is the difference between the value at time of purchase and the known future value. Following is a chart that shows how to find the present value of a stripped bond. I have included a few examples to illustrate the process of amortization as well as the price movements for different yield changes. Merely find the intersection of a yield and a maturity point and you will find the present value or price.

Cost of $100 Principal of Zero Coupon Bonds

Years	3%	4%	5%	6%	7%	8%	9%	10%	11%	12%
1	$97.09	$96.15	$95.24	$94.34	$93.46	$92.59	$91.74	$90.91	$90.09	$89.29
2	94.22	92.38	90.60	88.85	87.14	85.48	83.86	82.27	80.72	79.21
3	91.45	88.80	86.23	83.75	81.35	79.03	76.79	74.62	72.52	70.50
4	88.77	85.35	82.07	78.94	75.94	73.07	70.32	67.68	65.16	62.74
5	86.17	82.03	78.12	74.41	70.89	67.56	64.39	61.39	58.54	55.84
6	83.64	78.85	74.36	70.14	66.18	62.46	58.97	55.68	52.60	49.70
7	81.18	75.79	70.77	66.11	61.78	57.75	54.00	50.51	47.26	44.23
8	78.80	72.84	67.36	62.32	57.67	53.39	49.45	45.81	42.46	39.36
9	76.49	70.02	64.12	58.74	53.84	49.36	45.28	41.55	38.15	35.03
10	74.25	67.30	61.03	55.37	50.26	45.64	41.46	37.69	34.27	31.18
11	72.07	64.68	58.09	52.19	46.92	42.20	37.97	34.18	30.79	27.75
12	69.95	62.17	55.29	49.19	43.80	39.01	34.77	31.01	27.67	24.70
13	67.90	59.76	52.62	46.37	40.88	36.07	31.84	28.12	24.86	21.98
14	65.91	57.44	50.09	43.71	38.17	33.35	29.16	25.51	22.33	19.56
15	63.98	55.21	47.67	41.20	35.63	30.83	26.70	23.14	20.06	17.41
16	62.10	53.06	45.38	38.83	33.26	28.51	24.45	20.99	18.03	15.50
17	60.28	51.00	43.19	36.60	31.05	26.36	22.39	19.04	16.20	13.79
18	58.51	49.02	41.11	34.50	28.93	24.37	20.50	17.27	14.55	12.27
19	56.79	47.12	39.13	32.52	27.06	22.53	18.78	15.66	13.07	10.92
20	55.13	45.29	37.24	30.66	25.26	20.83	17.19	14.20	11.75	9.72
21	53.51	43.53	35.45	28.90	23.58	19.26	15.74	12.88	10.55	8.65
22	51.94	41.84	33.74	27.24	22.01	17.80	14.42	11.69	9.48	7.70
23	50.42	40.22	32.11	25.67	20.55	16.46	13.20	10.60	8.52	6.85
24	48.94	38.65	30.57	24.20	19.18	15.22	12.09	9.61	7.65	6.10
25	47.50	37.15	29.09	22.81	17.91	14.07	11.07	8.72	6.88	5.43

Let's work through these examples:

- Move to year 20 and across to the 5 percent column; there you find a value of $37.24. This is the present value of $100 due in twenty years at a semi-annually compounding yield of 5 percent.
- Staying with the 5 percent column, move up to year 15, where the value has amortized to $47.67; by year 10 it becomes $61.03; with 5 years left it becomes $78.12; at maturity it reaches $100. These prices represent the present value at 5 percent for those different maturities. This process is called amortization.
- Move to year 15 and the 4 percent column and you observe a price of $55.21. Now move over to the 7 percent column and you see that the value at that yield would be $35.63. Strip bonds rise and fall as interest rates change, but if held to maturity, they will reach that future value no matter where yields go in the interim.
- Go back to row 20 and the 5 percent yield column ($37.24). Now go to row 15 and 3 percent and you find $63.98. Wow, you say, my money has almost doubled in five years! Go across to the 5 percent column again and you find $47.67. That is what the amortized value would have been at 5 percent. The difference between $63.98 and $47.67 is the actual capital gain, with the balance of $10.43 being the amortized value.

Strips are that rarest of investment products: they are actually of benefit to individual investors, especially in the facilitation of retirement planning, while at the same time they answer IAs' biggest criticism of fixed-income products, low-percentage commissions. Strips generally produce 1 percent to 3 percent commission on average for IAs but still produce excellent yields for investors. At the same time they are an optimum choice for retirement planning, in that a finite future nominal value is known at the time of purchase.

Also remember our old friend reinvestment risk. There are no interest payments to reinvest, which we know can have a serious impact on actual or realized yield (or, if you prefer, on your ability to retire). Many of those regular payments or dividends are left idle, often being too small for investment in individual products. The appeal of strips is as investments that will grow to a precise future amount at an attractive yield and without any tiny amounts to worry about reinvesting.

Here are a couple of examples showing how investors could double or triple their money, in nominal future value, using $10,000 as a starting amount:

British Columbia 0 percent February 19, 2020, at $49.83, 4.82 percent. Future value: $10,000 / .4983 = $20,068.23.

Nova Scotia Power 0 percent August 26, 2028, at $31.48, 5.05 percent. Future value: $10,000 / .3148 = $31,766.20.

As retirement looms, more certainty is welcome. Stripped bonds ease the uncertainty by allowing investors to know exactly in nominal terms what their retirement pot will be worth.

Consider the case of a baby-boomer couple in their early fifties with an RRSP of $260,866; they are empty nesters and their children have repaid them for university. They still own real estate so they have an equity investment. Common shares and mutual funds have fluctuating market values with no certainty as to what their market value will be when the money is needed for retirement. Individual bonds have finite maturity dates but have all those bothersome semi-annual interest payments that clutter up the RRSP, often remaining uninvested.

The first example shows the future value of this couple's RRSP without any additional contributions using an actual ten-year stripped bond. Ontario Hydro 0 percent due November 26, 2015. Purchase price: $64.18 to yield 4.49 percent. Future value = $260,886 / .6418 = $ 406,491.

You say there is no guarantee what the purchasing power of that future value will be? Absolutely right! To guard against the possible erosion of this amount through inflation, what we do is revert to the laddered approach (mentioned already and explained in detail in the next chapter), which allows for annual reinvestment. The following portfolio sets out how such a portfolio would look today:

01-Dec-05

Issuer	Coupon	Maturity	Quantity	Price	S/A Yield	Ann Equiv	Total Value
Br. Col.	0.000%	18-Dec-06	$35,000.00	97.00	2.932%	2.953%	$33,950.00
Ontario	0.000%	02-Dec-07	$35,000.00	94.06	3.081%	3.105%	$32,921.00
Br. Col.	0.000%	18-Dec-08	$35,000.00	90.65	3.248%	3.275%	$31,727.50
Br. Col.	0.000%	18-Dec-09	$35,000.00	86.97	3.480%	3.510%	$30,439.50
Ontario	0.000%	02-Dec-10	$35,000.00	83.28	3.691%	3.725%	$29,148.00
Quebec	0.000%	01-Dec-11	$35,000.00	79.17	3.931%	3.970%	$27,709.50
Br. Col.	0.000%	18-Dec-12	$35,000.00	75.08	4.109%	4.151%	$26,278.00
Ontario	0.000%	02-Dec-13	$35,000.00	71.42	4.251%	4.296%	$24,997.00
Ontario	0.000%	02-Dec-14	$35,000.00	67.76	4.370%	4.418%	$23,716.00
Ont. Hydro	0.000%	26-Nov-15	$35,000.00	64.18	4.491%	4.541%	$22,463.00
			$350,000.00	Avg. Yield	3.752%	3.794%	$260,886.50

As you can see, the future value of this portfolio is exactly $350,000, $89,114 more than the amount this couple had to invest. This is a "sleep-at-night" portfolio. We could have chosen nothing but the 2015 year maturity, in which case the future value would have been much higher ($260,886 / .6418 = $406,491). However, choosing that route exposes these investors to reinvestment risk. Should rates rise sharply in intervening years, they would be at a disadvantage with no money to invest at those higher yields. However, by laddering the portfolio, a constant stream of maturities is available for reinvestment. The above total of $350,000 in future value thus understates what the final amount will be since each maturing coupon will be reinvested, adding to the future value. In the laddered strategy chapter, we will examine what this portfolio might look like a year later. This removes interest rate guessing from this couple's retirement planning. It contrasts sharply with a mutual bond fund, where the future value will not be known until the funds are needed and the investors have no control over maturity selection.

Thus, we have eliminated both types of reinvestment risk. There are no interest payments to reinvest, and the maturities are staggered to eliminate the risk of putting all the eggs in the wrong basket.

Now let us strip a bond. The market for stripped bonds is immense. As of May 31, 2005, there had been $82.8 billion in face value of bonds stripped with a resulting face value of strips outstanding of $185.2 billion. Trading is very active, averaging approximately $9.5 billion per month. Once again, we will use the Canada 5 percent due June 1, 2014. To strip these bonds we need another tool or two. For one, we need to know the Canada yield curve (the yield on Government of Canada bonds). You may wish to refresh your knowledge of the yield curve from the chapter "Basic Math." In any event, each interest payment when stripped will be sold at a yield relative to the yield on the Canada yield curve at a similar maturity. Thus, as the yield curve slopes upward, each interest payment would be sold or valued at progressively higher yields. The other significant variable here is the yield spread from the Canada yield curve to each future payment date. The curve and the spread in basis points that each payment would be valued as follows:

Zero Coupon Yield Curve

Term (years)	Canada Bond Yield	Spread to Zero Coupon Curve	Zero Coupon Yield
0.5	2.66	0.08	2.74
1.0	2.88	0.09	2.97
1.5	3.10	0.13	3.23
2.0	3.15	0.15	3.30
2.5	3.20	0.16	3.36
3.0	3.25	0.18	3.43
3.5	3.30	0.20	3.50
4.0	3.35	0.21	3.56
4.5	3.40	0.22	3.62
5.0	3.45	0.22	3.67
5.5	3.50	0.24	3.74
6.0	3.60	0.26	3.86
6.5	3.65	0.25	3.90
7.0	3.70	0.25	3.95
7.5	3.75	0.26	4.01
8.0	3.80	0.28	4.08
8.5	3.85	0.28	4.13

This spread is a function of several factors, including supply and demand, not only for the bond itself but also for the stripped bonds at different maturities. As well, the strippers need to make a profit. How do they do that? Applying the prevailing market spreads for the interest payments to each payment and adding up the pieces produces a present value either higher or lower than the cost of the bond. If the present value exceeds the cost, then the stripper sells the components separately and pockets the difference. In this example, the Canada yield curve is normal, or upward-sloping, and so the yields are progressively higher. You will note that every interest payment sold at a lower yield than the quoted yield to maturity of the bond in question (4 percent) produces a profit, while every payment sold at a higher yield produces a loss. As long as the net of the profits and losses is a profit, then the bond is stripped. The stripper does not care where the profit comes from. Following through with this thought, if the yield curve were perfectly flat (yields the same at all maturities), then most of the interest payments would have to be sold at a lower yield for the bond to be stripped profitably.

In the example below, in the first column is the present value of each payment at the purchase yield, in the second is the yield for Canada strips of that maturity, in the third is the price per $100 of that payment, and in the fourth column is the actual present value of each future payment. To the extent this value exceeds the 4 percent cost, there is a profit, as shown in the last column (losses are shown where the present value is less than cost). The net profit is calculated from the sum of all these calculations.

ZERO COUPON

Coupon Date	Zero Coupon Market Yield	Market Price	Value of $2,500 Coupon	Value at 4%	Profit/Loss
6/1/2006	2.74	98.650	$ 2,466.25	$ 2,450.98	$ 15.27
12/1/2006	2.97	97.095	$ 2,427.38	$ 2,402.92	$ 24.45
6/1/2007	3.23	95.307	$ 2,382.68	$ 2,355.80	$ 26.88
12/1/2007	3.30	93.664	$ 2,341.60	$ 2,309.62	$ 31.98
6/1/2008	3.36	92.007	$ 2,300.18	$ 2,264.33	$ 35.85
12/1/2008	3.43	90.300	$ 2,257.50	$ 2,219.93	$ 37.57
6/1/2009	3.50	88.564	$ 2,214.10	$ 2,176.40	$ 37.70
12/1/2009	3.56	86.836	$ 2,170.90	$ 2,133.73	$ 37.17
6/1/2010	3.62	85.091	$ 2,127.28	$ 2,091.90	$ 35.37
12/1/2010	3.67	83.374	$ 2,084.35	$ 2,050.88	$ 33.47
6/1/2011	3.74	81.563	$ 2,039.08	$ 2,010.65	$ 28.43
12/1/2011	3.86	79.502	$ 1,987.55	$ 1,971.22	$ 16.33
6/1/2012	3.90	77.798	$ 1,944.95	$ 1,932.58	$ 12.37
12/1/2012	3.95	76.048	$ 1,901.20	$ 1,894.70	$ 6.50
6/1/2013	4.01	74.247	$ 1,856.18	$ 1,857.52	-$ 1.35
12/1/2013	4.08	72.389	$ 1,809.73	$ 1,821.13	-$ 11.41
6/1/2014	4.10	70.824	$,770.60	$ 1,785.40	-$ 14.80
6/1/2014	4.10	70.824	$70,824.00	$71,416.00	-$592.00
Total			$106,905.48	$107,145.69	-$240.21

In this case, stripping $100,000 of this bond would have produced a loss of $240.21. As you can see, there was profit in all the coupons until June 1, 2013, after which the yields were higher than 4 percent, resulting in losses. You can see the importance of the principal (or residual) component. The stripper would not strip this bond unless the price of it fell suddenly or if he or she could sell the residual for a higher price.

Naturally, this raises questions. Why is there any profit in this? Wouldn't dealers or others arbitrage all the profit away? Any government bond can be stripped, simply by ensuring that the sum of the parts exceeds the cost; it is a sum-of-the-parts business. When an investment dealer strips a bond, it is usually a multi-million-dollar transaction, and not all of the pieces will be sold immediately. Typically, a stripper will calculate the break-even yields for the strip (i.e., yields at which the present values for the pieces equal the cost of the bond) and then compare those yields to the street bid side (i.e., what other investment dealers would pay for all the pieces) to calculate the bailout value of the strip. If that is marginally profitable, and the stripper believes that sufficient demand exists so that a high percentage of the strip could be sold at the ask side (i.e., the transfer price to the IAs), then the profitability is enhanced.

This is so since the spread between the bid and the ask is fairly wide in strips, typically 5 to 15 basis points depending on term, credit quality, and supply and demand. Since investment dealers carry large inventories of strips of all types and maturities, there are financing costs, hedging costs, spread risks, and yield curve risks to consider. Frequently, demand for strips may be weak or institutional and/or retail investors may be net sellers, which means that inventories swell. In that case, dealers make their products cheaper to lighten inventories, and with the wider spreads, new stripping is less profitable or not profitable until the overhang is cleaned up.

What happens if the selling continues? What can the investment dealer do? Well, believe it or not, particularly with Canada strips, they can be put back together or reconstituted and sold as regular bonds. Since most Canada bonds pay interest on June 1 and December 1, the Bank of Canada has made these coupon payments fungible, meaning that they can be added to any of the bonds with June 1 and December 1 interest payment dates. This makes the reconstitution process easier and adds efficiency to the stripped bond marketplace. Owing to numerous factors, such as foreign investors and new issues, anomalies appear that create stripping opportunities. As the strip market has matured and become more efficient, profit margins have been squeezed, but with the costs and risks associated with maintaining a large inventory, there is usually some gross profit visible in the strip market.

What happens if the yield curve is flat or inverted? The strip curve changes. In the case of the flat yield curve, the strips would be sold at lower yields than the Canada curve, while in an inverted yield curve environment, the strip profit would be in the longer maturities with losses at the front end.

Who are the buyers of strips? Strips are not suitable for taxable investors since the annual amortization of the strips counts as income and must be declared. Taxable investors would pay tax on income that they had not actually received! Thus, the sheltered plans (principally pension funds and RRSPs) dominate this market. However, there are other large investors who from time to time have a significant appetite for strips. Chartered banks and trust companies frequently invest GIC monies when mortgage demand is weak and strip yields are higher than GIC yields (a fairly frequent occurrence). Provincial sinking funds also make use of strips, as provincial governments are obliged to set aside funds for debt repayment. Strips are ideal for offsetting debt since they have a known future value. Insurance companies often balance assets and liabilities and fund structured settlement cases. The duration of long-term strips is valuable in matching long-term liabilities. Strips are also purchased by other non-profit organizations and foundations that do not need current income.

Virtually all the stripping activity involves federal and provincial bonds, although certain corporations (e.g., Bell Canada) have issued strips. The yields on the Canada strips trade at certain spreads from the Canada yield curve; provincial strips trade at differing spreads from the Canada strips, depending on credit rating, term, and supply and demand. Clearly if you believe the lesser rated provinces will honour their obligations, then some yield pickup is available.

There have been several strips done of Canadian issuers in U.S. dollars that are fully eligible for RRSPs without being considered foreign content. This, by the way, applies to any bond issued by a Canadian issuer in any currency. In addition, bonds or strips of certain supra-national borrowers, the most prominent of which is the World Bank, are also RRSP-eligible and not considered foreign content. The liquidity in these foreign currency strips is not good, so the bid-ask spread is wide and often there is no supply.

Let us digress for some history of the stripping business.

The Early Days of Stripping Bonds

This is a trip down memory lane. You have absorbed the importance of strips for retirement planning and how you can invest to the last dollar. It was not always so easy.

Stripping bonds began in Canada in 1981–2. In those days, we used hand-held calculators to work out the mathematics of stripping. A thirty-year bond becomes sixty-one separate securities (sixty semi-annual interest payments plus the principal) when stripped, and so we had to calculate the present value for each of them, add them all up, and see if the sum exceeded the cost of the bond, all the while hoping that the market would not move against us!

Back in those days, bonds were all in physical form, either registered in the owner's name or unregistered (a bearer bond). Thus, when stripping bonds, we actually used scissors to separate each coupon of a bearer bond from the others and from the principal portion (residue or residual). These coupons were not much bigger than a postage stamp and were bearer, which meant essentially that they were akin to cash, as they were payable on demand to the bearer at maturity or at the discounted market price before maturity. These small bearer instruments were an administrative nightmare!

The basis unit for stripping back then was $100,000 face value. Using a bond with a 5 percent semi-annual coupon for simplicity's sake, each individual coupon would have a face value of $2,500 ($100,000 * .05 / 2). The principal or residual portion, of course, had a face value of $100,000.

The primary investors were individual investors for their RRSPs and institutions such as pension funds and insurance companies that could match known liabilities by investing in strips to mature at the same time as the liability was due. Let us say that XYZ pension fund needed a $10-million strip maturing in thirty years. ABC investment dealer would ascertain the cost of buying the whole bond and then add up the present value of all the pieces, estimating where the various coupons could be sold. Happy with the sums, the dealer would proceed to strip the bonds. The "cage," or back office, then has to take the one hundred separate bonds (100 * $100,000 = $10 million), take the scissors to all of those little coupons, and stuff all of the $2,500 coupons into separate envelopes! They would then be put in a vault.

Then, of course, the dealer would begin to sell all of these envelopes (or parts of them) to investors of all kinds. If a retail investor wanted to purchase $10,000 face value, they would have to be removed from the envelope and segregated. The principal portion was thus highly prized, as it was a larger piece of paper (8 1/2" by 11") and was bigger in face value ($100,000), so it was easier for an investor to deploy larger amounts of money by buying the residual. As you could guess, the residuals were keenly sought after and commanded a significant premium over coupons of the same maturity. Illustrating this point, using the above example, the investment dealer would have to strip $400 million of bonds to create enough coupons to provide the $10 million face value.

Also, in those days, many institutional investors required physical delivery to their addresses, be they in Victoria or Halifax, or to their custodian (trust company). You can conjure up the image of armoured trucks criss-crossing the country stuffed full of these envelopes. The recipients, of course, would then have to stuff them in their own vaults. You can imagine the fun trying to keep all of this straight and trying to keep track of maturing coupons. One of the most prominent zero coupon buyers practically ran out of room and was partly responsible for the change to a book-based system.

I can remember taking a flight to Halifax with $45 million of bearer residuals in my bag in order not to miss settlement by a day! I collected the cheque and took my client to lunch.

This administrative nightmare did not go unnoticed. Eventually, the investment business gave birth to a zero coupon product derived from physical bonds. These bore names such as Tigrs, Sentinels, and Cougars (to name the most prominent). A block of bonds was taken and registered in a trust company's name. There were no coupons; rather, a cheque was sent to the trust company as each coupon or residual matured. The trustee would then distribute the proceeds on a proportional basis to the registered owners. Investors received nice, fancy, big pieces of paper telling them that they owned the relevant portion of the underlying bond. There were two types: alter-ego, which meant that the investor could only buy the actual face value of the coupon in question (or a multiple thereof), and non-alter-ego, which meant that each underlying coupon could be sold in fractions as long as all the fractions added up to the appropriate face value.

This approach saved countless headaches and costs at the retail level, but many institutions could not buy them because of their investment by-laws, so they never really took a significant percentage of the stripped bond business. Once the industry moved to a book-based system, these derived instruments traded at a healthy discount from conventional strips.

Eventually, book-based stripping evolved to where the bonds are held by the trustee for CDS and no physical stripping is done. It is all computer blips now, so the need for these alternative evidences of ownership disappeared. However, there are millions outstanding, and investment dealers make markets in them as well.

Summary for Zero Coupon Bonds

We know that the value of a bond is nothing more than the sum of its parts. Obviously \$1 due in twenty years is not worth \$1 today. What is it worth? Discounting it at an interest rate or yield to determine its worth, applying this discount rate to that future value, and employing the present value formula produces the answer. Thus, \$100,000 due in twenty years discounted at a semi-annual yield of 5 percent produces a present value of \$37,243. Expressed in reverse, \$37,423 invested at 5 percent semi-annually will grow or compound to $100,000 in twenty years. Where does this yield or discount rate come from? In the case of the stripped bond market, it is a function of the yields for the Canada curve at that maturity, supply and demand for strips, and the mathematics of stripping.

Zero coupon bonds are a very important retirement planning tool. As retirement moves closer, investors require more certainty, and strips offer that. Furthermore, they can be rolled into a RRIF easily and would not have to be sold. A laddered strip portfolio will serve investors well by taking away reinvestment risk and still providing precise future values, all the time being invested in high quality, primarily government, securities. Just imagine: a high quality, fully compounding investment product that is ideally suited for retirement planning!

CHAPTER SIX

Building a Ladder to Success, or Why a Portfolio of Individual Fixed-income Securities Is In Your Best Interest

I was a portfolio manager for two of Canada's most prominent financial organizations, managing billions of dollars of other people's money in the form of life insurance, pension funds, and mutual funds. I invested the first dollar for what is now Canada's largest public mutual bond fund (Investor's Bond Fund) in 1979. It is worth remembering as you read this chapter that I have a balanced perspective on both individual fixed-income securities and mutual bond funds.

Laddering

There is a tried-and-true strategy for fixed-income investing that ensures above-average results. It is called the laddered or staggered-maturity strategy. Simply, this involves dividing a given sum of money into equal portions and investing these portions in bonds of regularly spaced maturities. For example, assuming an amount of $250,000, one could divide this into ten amounts of $25,000 and invest each amount in maturities of one year, two years, all the way to ten years.

What is the rationale for such a strategy? First, it eliminates the risk of having all the money invested in a single maturity, thus avoiding the possibility of having to reinvest it a lower rate upon maturity. Second, it takes the guesswork out of interest rates. No one money manager has ever consistently and accurately forecast the direction of interest rates. The laddered strategy takes away the guesswork since there is always something about to mature for reinvestment while the rest of the funds are spread out in the various maturities. The net effect is to smooth out long-term returns and avoid the yield traps, as I discussed in the yield curve section. Third, it allows for diversification by issuer, thus reducing credit risk.

Sticking with our one- to ten-year ladder example, when the one-year bond matures, that money is reinvested in a ten-year bond since the previous ten-year bond now has a nine-year term to maturity. Examples following will illustrate this. Also, since this is a buy-and-hold strategy, provincial and corporate bonds should be used, and enhanced compound yield will result. This is because Government of Canada bonds, the most liquid, are also the lowest yielding, and you do not need the liquidity in a buy-and-hold portfolio. The extra yield from investing in higher yielding provincials and corporates will compound over time to provide a greater retirement amount. Here is an example of what a laddered portfolio looks like.

01-Dec-05

Laddered Bond Portfolio

Quantity	Issuer	Coupon	Maturity	Price	S/A Yield	Ann Equiv	Total Value
$25,000	Cdn. Cap. Auto Rec.	3.478%	17-Nov-06	100.29	3.17%	3.19%	$25,105.85
$25,000	Encana	5.300%	03-Dec-07	103.85	3.30%	3.33%	$26,619.55
$25,000	Manulife	4.300%	22-Dec-08	102.24	3.52%	3.55%	$26,037.12
$25,000	Merrill CDA	4.200%	08-Dec-09	101.96	3.67%	3.70%	$25,996.30
$25,000	Farm Credit	3.500%	15-Oct-10	99.16	3.69%	3.72%	$24,902.67
$25,000	Man. Tel	5.200%	27-Sep-11	104.85	4.25%	4.29%	$26,444.01
$25,000	Ontario	5.375%	02-Dec-12	108.90	3.91%	3.95%	$27,895.03
$30,000	Loblaws	5.400%	20-Nov-13	106.70	4.39%	4.44%	$32,058.82
$30,000	Royal Bank	4.710%	22-Dec-14	102.75	4.34%	4.39%	$31,452.14
$30,000	Royal Bank	4.250%	03-Dec-15	100.40	4.20%	4.24%	$30,752.26

Total Cost Including Accrued Interest **$246,511.50**

Weighted Average Semi-annual Yield	4.360%
Average Coupon	4.571%
Weighted Average Term	6.41 years

Total Annual Income **$12,146.25**

Let us examine this portfolio. You will notice there are no Government of Canada bonds in it. Since this portfolio is not going to be actively traded, there is no point in investing in the lowest-yielding bonds in the bond market when there are good-quality provincial and corporate issues available that offer higher yield that will compound in your favour (remember the compound yield section). The average maturity of this portfolio is 6.41 years. The most important feature is that the maturities span the length of approximately two business cycles. This portfolio will likely outperform the majority of professional fund managers because you are not paying annual management fees, you hold no Canadas, and you are not guessing which way interest rates are going.

As time passes and your first bond matures, you invest in another ten-year bond that meets your standards, and so on with each maturity. This means that you are never concentrated in one maturity, where you would be at risk if rates were very low; you must reinvest at prevailing rates and accept the average yields. There are variations on this theme, of course. Some investors prefer short-term ladders, others long-term, and some have maturities every second year. You can also invest a percentage in foreign pay securities should you desire currency diversification. As well, some investors may wish to put, say, 75 percent of their portfolio into a laddered configuration and deploy the balance where they feel the maximum returns may be obtained.

Over time, this approach has outperformed the majority of professional fund managers for the essential reasons that there is no guesswork involved, no annual management fees, and the funds are invested in bonds yielding more than Canadas. It is true that fees on individual fixed-income transactions average 1 percent, but note that for the above example only 10 percent of the portfolio matures annually, so in effect, investors pay annual fees of only one-tenth of 1 percent compared with the average MER of 1.8 percent for managed bond funds.

The ladder provides an investor with specific maturing amounts at specific dates. It permits investors to avoid the all important reinvestment risk of having all their money invested in the wrong maturity.

This strategy can be applied to both taxable accounts and retirement accounts. For RRSPs, a stripped-bond ladder may be used (see previous chapter as well as below), while interest-bearing bonds are normally employed in the taxable account. A younger investor may choose a long-term ladder. If investors are not starting with enough money for a complete ladder, they can select individual rungs, nicely spaced out, and fill in the gaps as funds become available. For instance, with $20,000 investors could begin by investing $10,000 in a one-year bond and the other $10,000 in a ten-year bond, then perhaps add a five-year maturity later, and so on. Laddering offers investors a great deal of flexibility and customization.

How do you choose the rungs on the ladder? If you have found a good IA, his or her organization should have an extensive inventory from which to choose. If you are dealing with an online or discount broker, they should provide the tools to enable you to construct such a portfolio yourself. Your aim should be to choose the highest yielding bonds for each rung that meet your credit quality threshold. The issue of credit quality is an important one and was addressed in the corporate bond section.

This approach is also important in RRSPs. Even though the plan is sheltered, the same investment principles apply, except that you would build a ladder of strips; since strips can be rolled into an RRIF, there is no compelling need to concentrate maturities at retirement age. Consider the following RRSP laddered portfolio, repeated from Chapter 5, constructed for a typical boomer couple. Assume that they are in their early fifties, empty nesters, their children have repaid them for their university costs, and they have a combined RRSP of $260,886.

The total of $350,000 in future value understates what the final amount will be, since each maturing coupon will be reinvested and will add to the future value. This removes interest rate guessing from this couple's retirement planning and allows them to sleep at night. This contrasts sharply with a mutual bond fund where the future value will not be known until their funds are needed and where the investors have no control over maturity selection.

01-Dec-05

Issuer	Coupon	Maturity	Quantity	Price	S/A Yield	Ann Equiv	Total Value
Br. Col.	0.000%	18-Dec-06	$35,000.00	97.00	2.932%	2.953%	$33,950.00
Ontario	0.000%	02-Dec-07	$35,000.00	94.06	3.081%	3.105%	$32,921.00
Br. Col.	0.000%	18-Dec-08	$35,000.00	90.65	3.248%	3.275%	$31,727.50
Br. Col.	0.000%	18-Dec-09	$35,000.00	86.97	3.480%	3.510%	$30,439.50
Ontario	0.000%	02-Dec-10	$35,000.00	83.28	3.691%	3.725%	$29,148.00
Quebec	0.000%	01-Dec-11	$35,000.00	79.17	3.931%	3.970%	$27,709.50
Br. Col.	0.000%	18-Dec-12	$35,000.00	75.08	4.109%	4.151%	$26,278.00
Ontario	0.000%	02-Dec-13	$35,000.00	71.42	4.251%	4.296%	$24,997.00
Ontario	0.000%	02-Dec-14	$35,000.00	67.76	4.370%	4.418%	$23,716.00
Ont. Hydro	0.000%	26-Nov-15	$35,000.00	64.18	4.491%	4.541%	$22,463.00
			$350,000.00	Avg. Yield	3.752%	3.794%	$260,886.50

Here is what this portfolio might look like one year later:

01-Dec-06

Issuer	Coupon	Maturity	Quantity	Price	S/A Yield	Ann Equiv	Total Value
Ontario	0.000%	02-Dec-07	$35,000.00	96.98	3.082%	3.105%	$33,943.00
Br. Col.	0.000%	18-Dec-08	$35,000.00	93.62	3.248%	3.274%	$32,767.00
Br. Col.	0.000%	18-Dec-09	$35,000.00	90.02	3.481%	3.511%	$31,507.00
Ontario	0.000%	02-Dec-10	$35,000.00	86.38	3.692%	3.726%	$30,233.00
Quebec	0.000%	01-Dec-11	$35,000.00	82.31	3.932%	3.970%	$28,808.50
Br. Col.	0.000%	18-Dec-12	$35,000.00	78.20	4.108%	4.151%	$27,370.00
Ontario	0.000%	02-Dec-13	$35,000.00	74.48	4.252%	4.297%	$26,068.00
Ontario	0.000%	02-Dec-14	$35,000.00	70.75	4.371%	4.419%	$24,762.50
Ont. Hydro	0.000%	26-Nov-15	$35,000.00	67.09	4.491%	4.542%	$23,481.50
Manitoba	0.000%	05-Sep-16	$54,816.00	63.85	4.650%	4.704%	$35,000.02
			$369,816.00	Avge. Yield	3.931%	3.970	$293,940.52

What has happened is that the B.C. due December 18, 2006, matured and the proceeds of $35,000 were invested in the Manitoba September 5, 2016 maturity. With that zero coupon being offered at a price of .6385, this couple could buy $54,816 of face value ($35,000 / .6385). Now the total future value is $369,816. Also note that the total value of the portfolio has risen to $293,940 by virtue of reinvesting the full $35,000, and all of the other zero coupons are one year closer to maturity. This means that their present value has increased (I held the yields constant year-to-year to make this point). This process will be repeated annually until the couple chooses one future date for their monies to mature and they buy strips to mature on that date. Strips can be held past age seventy-one and can be used for RRIF payments.

The laddered approach is a tried-and-true approach to fixed-income investing and is in your best interest. It is simple, easy to implement, and leads to above-average results. Better yet, it is a strategy that you can implement yourself.

Why Not Mutual Bond Funds?

Let us re-examine the differences between individual fixed-income products and mutual bond funds.

Mutual fixed-income funds or bond funds never mature. Investors do not know what their funds will be worth in the future. Why is this? Portfolio managers are paid to manage portfolios, and they are paid handsomely. The typical management expense ratio is 1.5 percent to 2 percent per year, and is charged to the fund. Therefore at the start of any year you are already behind the starting line. Put another way, if a bond fund produces 5 percent, and fees are 1.5 percent, the net returns will be 3.5 percent. The fund managers will attempt to recoup that management fee by brilliantly outperforming all the other fund managers. You will thus receive outstanding returns after the management fee is deducted from the fund's returns. Of course, they still collect if performance is subpar or negative!

So, how does one portfolio manager outperform the peer group? Luck and guesswork, mostly. You may come across the expression "rate anticipation trading," which describes this approach. It means guessing which way bond prices are going and positioning the portfolio accordingly. Sounds easy. Interest rates are about to climb, so sell the entire portfolio, go into treasury bills, and preserve capital while at least earning money market returns. Then, just when interest rates have reached their peak, invest the entire portfolio into the longest term bonds and reap substantial capital gains plus the income minus the management fee. Does this ever happen? Rarely! The majority of fixed-income fund managers fret and tug at their locks as they attempt to have their portfolios closely track the relevant bond index with enough difference to have slightly better performance than their peer group. No one fixed-income portfolio manager has ever gotten it right all the time.

Also consider that bond funds are required to calculate an annual return since they do not have a fixed maturity date. Investors owning individual bonds do not have to worry about annual returns since their yield and maturity date are known at the time of purchase. Remember the analogy of a baseball game. Individual investors in specific fixed-income securities know the outcome of the game before it starts even though the score, or annual return, may vary inning by inning. Bond fund holders have to worry every inning since they may have to leave the stadium before the end of the game without knowing what the score will be!

The majority of fund managers are doomed to be average because no one gets it right every time. They care less about how well your money is doing than they do about their relative performance, on which their bonuses hinge. Few investment organizations demand a positive return before considering bonuses. Independent performance measurement companies assemble a universe of data, producing results comparing all the fund managers by results over different time periods. The data is broken down into four sections called quartiles, with the point between the second and third quartiles called the median. Every manager wants to be consistently in the second quartile or higher, and better than the bond index. It does not matter if the bond market is in a tailspin with negative returns. If the bond market's total performance was -10 percent and Portfolio Manager X was at -8 percent and the bond index wad at -9 percent, the manager gets to keep his/her job with a possible performance bonus!

In my experience, people I meet with funds invested in bond funds have no idea what securities are in those funds. It is possible to review carefully the quarterly (sometimes semi-annual) statements when they are released, eight or so weeks after the period ends. Unfortunately, it is only a snapshot, but hardly anyone looks anyway. There is no way to tell whether the fund manager totally changed the structure of the fund in the meantime. As well, there may have been a new fund manager appointed with a different investment philosophy who could have made significant changes to the portfolio without your knowledge.

It is safe to say that it is extremely unlikely for an individual's unique investment objectives to be met by any fund manager who has relative performance as the top criterion, rather than the individual investment objectives of thousands of unit holders. You may request the quarterly transactions of your portfolio manager — not a widely advertised fact — to better understand what is happening to your money.

There are attempts to analyze and compare fixed-income funds for the investing public. The *Financial Post*, every three months, breaks out the composition of the funds into their various categories and other details, namely the average term and the percentage held in cash reserves, Canadas, provincials, corporates, strips, and foreign currency bonds. While only a snapshot and hopelessly out of date, it does reveal a lot about the investment strategies and philosophies of the different investment organizations. A high percentage in cash means the fund manager expects interest rates to rise and is defending the unit value of the fund, since there is no market risk in short-term treasury bills. Conversely, fund performance would suffer if interest rates were to fall, since the portion of the fund invested in the money market would not appreciate in value. A high percentage held in Canadas may give you a warm, safe feeling, but be aware that they are the lowest yielding securities in the Canadian bond universe. In order to compensate for this lower yield, portfolio managers trade Canadas actively and aggressively, carrying out rate anticipation trading (guessing), switches, and yield curve plays. It is a big casino, folks! While a certain percentage of Canadas may be needed for liquidity purposes, a consistently high concentration in Canadas means that high-risk trading practices are employed with a strong possibility of poor performance. If the bulk of the fund is instead invested in higher yielding provincials and corporates, that extra yield compounds in the unit holder's favour, making it harder for the "guessers" to keep pace. Of course the guessers are not always right, and this makes the gap even wider.

Belatedly, certain investment organizations are making more special-purpose fixed-income funds available to allow investors more opportunities to tailor make their portfolios. There are now short-term government funds, corporate funds, zero-coupon funds, and high-yield (or junk) funds. In this case you may find these funds suitable, as the returns may be high enough to make it acceptable to pay the management fees.

Another investment vehicle alternative to bond mutual funds that investors may find attractive are exchange traded funds (ETFs). These are open-ended mutual fund trusts, and they trade on the TSX just like equities do. The two that are listed on the TSX are iG5 and ibond. The iG5 fund, managed by Barclays Global Investors, replicates as close as possible the performance of Government of Canada five-year bonds. The iBond fund, also managed by Barclay's, is also known by its full name, iUnits Canadian Bond Broad Market Index. Trading on the TSX under the stock symbol XBB, this fund replicates the Scotia Capital Universe Bond Index, thus offering investors exposure to a diversified portfolio of bonds of different quality, maturity, and yield. They pay quarterly interest and annual capital gains distributions. The MER is only .30 percent, compared with the average of 1.8 percent for managed bond funds. Investors can lock in the yield on a five-year with a low MER. Sure beats the funds! You can learn more about ETFs at iunits.com.

The point of this is to underline the importance of identifying your own objectives and then matching those needs to the appropriate mutual funds.

Summary of Differences

- Bond funds never mature.
- Annual management fees make it difficult to achieve above-average returns.
- Funds cannot be tailored to individual needs.

Income Trusts, Royalty Trusts, and Real Estate Investment Trusts

Earlier in the book, I made reference to the fact that I hear from a lot of investors who yearn for the day when bond yields were in double-digit territory. I point out to these people, and to everyone else, that the real return on bonds (nominal yield minus inflation) is the same now with yields at 4 percent and inflation at 1.5 percent as it was when yields were 11 percent and inflation was 8.5 percent. That is, it is 2.5 percent.

I also point out to everyone that when investors buy bonds, they receive a fixed stream of income and a specific date in the future when they receive their principal back. Thus, bonds or fixed-income securities are cornerstones for investment and retirement planning.

However, investors continue to be greedy for higher yields. The investment business is reliable in inventing new products or approaches to perpetuate itself. After the collapse of the tech bubble and the drying up of Initial Public Offerings (IPOs) in 2000, investment bankers needed a new source of revenue and turned to the income trust business.

I do not intend to discuss these investments in any depth here for two basic reasons. First, they are not fixed-income securities. Rather, they are an equity investment with higher yields than common shares. Second, others have written books on nothing but this subject (see *Canadian Income Funds* by Bach and Romano).

However, I recognize that this book would not be complete without some discussion of them. At present, there are more than 112 business trusts trading on the TSX, with a market value in excess of $ 38 billion, and just recently, Standard and Poor indicated that they were planning to include a select list of trusts in their index.

One of the best analogies that I have heard regarding income trusts compares them to high-yield or junk bonds. Unlike investment-grade bonds, high-yield bonds have a lot of risk attached, with considerable uncertainty with respect to the repayment of principal. In other words, they are a lot like an equity investment.

Building a Ladder to Success

Remember, one of the all-time great maxims of the investment business is "Bulls make money, bears make money, but pigs get slaughtered." If investors are shifting money from equities to income trusts, that is fine. If they are moving funds from traditional fixed-income securities to trusts just for the higher apparent yield, then they will likely suffer the pigs' fate. Returns on trusts have been impressive, to be sure, but at unsustainable levels. Something will change: yields in the bond market may rise, Canada may go into recession, oil prices could plummet, governments could change the tax rules, or pension funds could drive prices up and yields down.

Investors must understand that trusts are equity-like securities with the attendant risks. They are not a substitute for fixed-income securities.

CHAPTER SEVEN
Attention GIC Shoppers!

Canadian investors have a love affair with guaranteed investment certificates (GICs). As of April 30, 2005, they owned $251 billion of GICs, of which $81.2 billion was in RRSPs. Why is this? For one, they are safe, being issued primarily by Canada's Schedule A chartered banks and other financial intermediaries. For another, the Canadian Deposit and Insurance Corporation (CDIC), a federal Crown corporation, guarantees each GIC of five years or less to maturity up to a maximum of $100,000. This was just raised from

$60,000 in the 2005 federal budget, retroactive to February 23, 2005. Investors can buy GICs from different banks to increase this amount. What features do GICs have? They are normally offered in terms from one year to five years with reasonable, not great, yields. They are not liquid and so are held to maturity. Again, why are they so popular? Because they are "sold" to investors by their banks. Why do banks issue GICS? To borrow money cheaply to reinvest in higher yielding securities.

GICs and RRSPs Are Not the Same Thing!

How often have you heard, or how often have you said, "I am going to my bank to buy my RRSPs?" or something similar, such as, "My RRSPs were only 5 percent this year." A whole generation of Canadians is convinced that an RRSP and a GIC are the same thing — as if an RRSP was an actual security or investment itself. Why has this happened? Why does this generation not know that they are subsidizing the issuers of GICs, who merely take your RRSP deposit and lend it out at higher rates? Why not get that higher rate yourself, or at least examine the other investment choices you have that can make your retirement pot that much bigger?

An RRSP is not an individual security or investment. It is a plan; that is what the "P" stands for. It is a plan that provides a medium through which you may choose from a diverse group of securities. One of the prime reasons why Canadians are seduced into the GIC/RRSP trap is the inertia of human nature. It is far easier to "buy" your RRSP from your branch manager than to set up a self-administered plan, choose an IA, and select the appropriate securities given your individual needs and objectives. There isn't much at stake here — only your retirement well-being!

To put this in more graphic terms, the size of the GIC market is $251 billion, of which approximately $45 billion matures within one year. That equates to $120 million per day! Of this total, an estimated $81.2 billion is held by RRSP accounts. Assuming that the institutions gathering these deposits are able to reinvest at rates 1 to 2 percent higher than they pay for the GICs, all the RRSP/GIC holders together are giving away in excess of $2 billion every year! This money would be better used for their retirement needs.

The astute readers will argue that an individual is unable to lend money in the same markets that the institutions do: the mortgage markets and the personal loan market. This is true. However, there are publicly traded securities that, at different stages of the interest cycle, provide higher yield than do GICs: government bonds, corporate bonds, stripped bonds, and mortgage-backed securities, to name a few. Even investing at an extra one-half of 1 percent would produce an extra $250 million annually for the RRSP holders of GICs and $750 million for all the GIC holders combined.

As at July 5, 2005

Term	GICs	Canada Bonds	Provincial Bonds	Corporate Bonds	Provincial Strips
3 years	2.40%	3.15%	3.25%	3.50%	3.20%
4 years	2.65%	3.35%	3.45%	4.10%	3.50%
5 years	2.95%	3.50%	3.70%	4.15%	3.70%
10 years	N/A	4.00%	4.20%	4.70%	4.50%

All yields annual equivalent

Ladders Versus GICs

Assuming a ten-year ladder, as in the previous example, we will demonstrate the long-term advantages accruing to those investors who heretofore have put all their faith in their bank or trust company manager and therefore all their money into GICs. As you know, they are seldom sold with a term greater than five years, which coincides with the longest mortgage term typically available. (Amazing coincidence. Just what do you think they did with your capital? Of course they loan it at much higher rates.) We are trying to get you some of those higher rates and better returns, which will lead to a happier retirement. The ladder illustrated has an average term of 6.41 years so you are no more exposed than if you owned a five-year GIC. What you have is a higher yield — 4.41 percent annual versus 2.95 percent — less investment risk, and excellent liquidity. The yield is higher because half of the portfolio is invested in the six- to ten-year terms, where yields are significantly greater than at five years, while you have short-term securities available for reinvestment. In the last two economic cycles, you would have earned an additional yield of approximately 100 basis points, which translates into a lot of dollars for a typical investor. An extra 1 percent over thirty years on an annual contribution of $13,500 would produce an extra $69,291. Also, these are all high-quality, marketable instruments.

Even more important, this whole GIC thing flies in the face of proper long-term investment planning. GICs are a narrow asset class, limited as to maturity and marketability, and therefore only suitable for a small percentage of one's portfolio. See the sections on reinvestment risk and laddered portfolios for a more complete analysis.

Providing for one's long-term retirement with short-term assets such as GICs is very risky.

The following portfolio is the same one seen in the chapter on laddered portfolios. The purpose of presenting it again is to point out the extra yield and, therefore, the income available by taking advantage of the fact that normally yields at longer maturities are higher than shorter term ones. At the same time, no extra risk is taken since the

01-Dec-05

Laddered Bond Portfolio

Quantity	Issuer	Coupon	Maturity	Price	S/A Yield	Ann Equiv	Total Cost
$25,000	Cdn. Cap. Auto Rec.	3.478%	17-Nov-06	100.29	3.17%	3.19%	$25,105.85
$25,000	Encana	5.300%	03-Dec-07	103.85	3.30%	3.33%	$26,619.55
$25,000	Manulife	4.300%	22-Dec-08	102.24	3.52%	3.55%	$26,037.12
$25,000	Merrill CDA	4.200%	08-Dec-09	101.96	3.67%	3.70%	$25,996.30
$25,000	Farm Credit	3.500%	15-Oct-10	99.16	3.69%	3.72%	$24,902.67
$25,000	Man. Tel	5.200%	27-Sep-11	104.85	4.25%	4.29%	$26,444.01
$25,000	Ontario	5.375%	02-Dec-12	108.90	3.91%	3.95%	$27,895.03
$30,000	Loblaws	5.400%	20-Nov-13	106.70	4.39%	4.44%	$32,058.82
$30,000	Royal Bank	4.710%	22-Dec-14	102.75	4.34%	4.39%	$31,452.14
$30,000	Royal Bank	4.250%	03-Dec-15	100.40	4.20%	4.24%	$30,752.26

Total Cost Including Accrued Interest **$246,511.50**

Weighted Average Semi-annual Yield	4.360%
Average Coupon	4.571%
Weighted Average Term	6.41 years

Total Annual Income **$12,146.25**

portfolio is laddered, and the average term of this portfolio is almost the same as a five-year GIC except that the average yield is higher than GICs at the time the portfolio was constructed. This is not a fluke; it is typical of the yield advantage available from five to ten years.

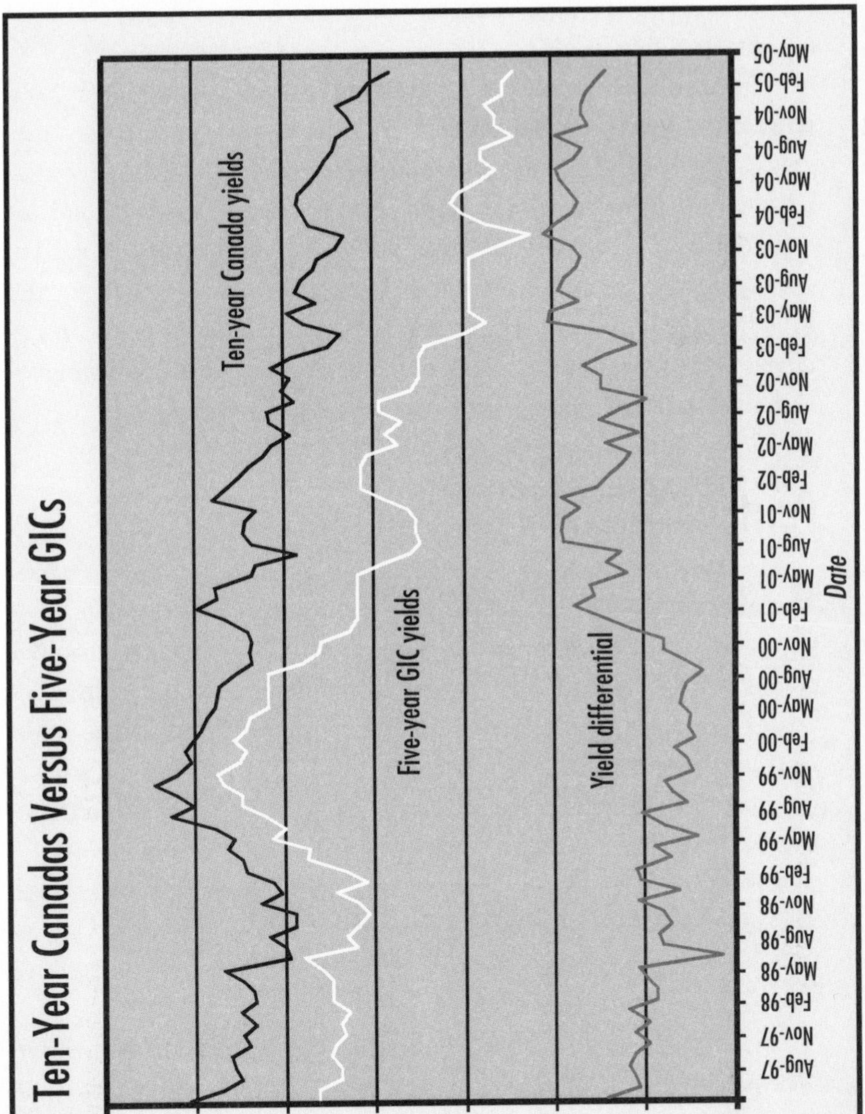

Ten-year Canadas have averaged 1.2 percent more than five-year GICs since 1997. Substituting higher yielding provincials, corporates, or strips would increase this yield advantage even more. This makes investment sense and produces significant monetary gains. Of course, the securities are all high quality and marketable so that the portfolio could be altered to suit changing needs or circumstances or to take advantage of better-yielding securities as they become available.

Think of your RRSP as a medium through which you create your retirement nest egg rather than your annual tax deferral that comes dressed up as a GIC. Once you shed the inertia and actually set up a self-directed retirement savings plan, what then? Stripped bonds or zero coupons frequently offer equal or higher yield than do GICs, have excellent quality and marketability, and are not subject to the $100,000 CDIC limit. Of course, strips are available in maturities as long as forty years and are totally free of reinvestment risk, allowing for better balance and superior long-term returns.

Portfolio Selection

There are thousands of bonds outstanding, issued by a variety of entities with varying features such as coupon, maturity, currency, call features, etc. How do you decide which ones to include in your portfolio? This process seems daunting, but by using a good IA and following a few rules, the process need not be arduous.

First, you are encouraged to reread the reinvestment risk section; it is key to security selection. Should you be constructing a portfolio that is either sheltered or taxable, the same rules apply but the types of securities will vary. For example, all you will be considering for your RRSP are strips while your taxable portfolio will consist only of income-bearing instruments.

All right, you have been patiently waiting to find out which securities to buy. Rule number one is what not to buy: avoid callable bonds. Individuals poring through weekend bond quotations are drawn to the highest yielding bonds. These bonds, in almost every instance, contain a feature or features that could result in your investment being called from you. There could be a financial call where the issuer may redeem the bonds and issue them at lower rates. As well, they may be low-quality credits where your capital may be at risk. This is hardly in your best interest and is yet another example of reinvestment risk! There is little point in carefully assembling a laddered portfolio only to have several rungs removed when the purpose of the ladder is to eliminate the possibility of having to reinvest your money when you do not want to (i.e., when rates are low). Some corporate bonds may also be called for sinking fund purposes, where the company buys back a certain percentage of a bond issue every year. In those cases you might not have all your bonds called but you will still have a reinvestment decision and your ladder will be all messed up.

Most bonds issued today are either non-callable for their entire life or callable at much narrower spreads than they were issued at. This latter type of call feature is commonly found on corporate issues. Let us return to the example of the recent Bell Canada 5.50 percent August 12, 2010, issued at $99.678 to yield 5.55 percent, 70 basis points over the Canada yield curve. Bell Canada may wish to call these bonds back at some point for corporate reasons. What has evolved in the market is that in order to call these bonds, the issuer would have to pay the higher of 100 or, in this case, at a yield spread of 17.5 basis points over the Canada yield curve. While the investors would lose their investment, they would receive a relative improvement of 52.5 basis points. This would mean a price of $108.75 to yield 3.605 percent today. They would still have to reinvest the money, but this is a friendlier call feature than the old style. Of course, your investment advisor will know which issues are callable and which ones are not.

Rule number two is stick to investment-grade securities, which are rated BBB or higher. Rating agencies constantly analyze issuers' credit worthiness. Investing in less than investment-grade bonds is more risky and requires constant research and due diligence.

The prime purpose of this chapter is to underscore the fact that a GIC and an RRSP are two different things. You can obtain greater returns through a number of other investment choices and approaches. In the fixed income world, zero coupons and laddered portfolios are two such vehicles.

CHAPTER EIGHT
Bonds for the Speculator

Bond prices change minute by minute. Daily price fluctuations for longer term bonds (five years and longer) can range from pennies to dollars, with the average daily change approximating fifty cents. The margin rate (the amount you need to put down) can be as low as 4 percent for Canada bonds with a term of three years and longer. You can see that it is possible to make or lose money quickly on twenty-five-times leverage! The margin rate of only 4 percent compares to 50 percent for most equities. Why is it so low? Because of the very high quality of fixed-income instruments, in addition to their liquidity. Also, bonds pay interest, typically at a higher rate than the cost of borrowing, so they have what we call a "positive" carry (i.e., the interest accruing on the bond exceeds the cost of borrowing on margin).

"Pro" trading, which involves borrowing money for the express purpose of creating capital gains from trading bonds, is confined largely to traders at the largest investment dealers; however, I have dealt with many well-heeled and informed individuals who have enjoyed success trading the bond market on margin. As with the equity markets, there are both fundamental and technical approaches to forecasting the direction of bond prices. Bond traders use both. Often it is relatively easy to observe the general direction of bond prices, but close attention to technical analysis can identify some short-term trading opportunities. The rest of this chapter will deal with technical analysis.

Just to be sure that my message is clear, I am including this chapter for the following reasons. First, the technical analysis of the direction of bond prices is important to investors in general. You now know that bond prices are always changing and can experience dramatic price movements. It is in your best interest to arm yourself with some technical tools to better time your purchases or sales. Using technical analysis can save you a lot of money, or to put it another way, it can add incremental yield to your portfolio. Second, technical analysis for bonds may be used by speculators for capital gains purposes. As I mentioned above, the margin rate for bonds is very low because of their quality so speculators are able to leverage their investments.

The following section walks you through the process of creating and using your own charts; you can build your own charts in spreadsheets, buy some software, or ask IAs to provide their firms' technical research. Or you can visit the Bank of Canada's wonderful website, which offers a plethora of interest rates and yields.

Again, careful monitoring of bond charts can help in the timing of an investment decision and can add to yield.

The average daily fluctuation of a long-term bond (ten-year and longer) has been approximately one half a point for the last ten years. Combine this fact with the very low margin requirements required to finance bonds and you have a potent combination for astute traders and speculators. Of course, in volatility there is opportunity and risk. There are savvy investors who chart bond prices and familiarize themselves with all the factors that produce short- and medium-term price changes for bonds. This is not for the faint of heart, folks. At a 10 percent margin, for example, leverage works in reverse in a hurry! For the sophisticated investor who is plugged into a bond desk or has a very competent IA, there are plenty of opportunities to employ this leverage for capital gains. Using margin to build a leveraged bond position also multiplies the commission, and since leveraged speculative bond positions are usually actively traded, this leads to repeat business for the IA.

My advice here is not to trade on margin unless you can buy $1 million face value of bonds. While the minimum margin required is only 4 percent for long-term government bonds, most investment dealers will ask for 10 percent margin to allow a cushion against minor price changes; speculators may wish to put down even a higher minimum to avoid margin calls and then maybe run that down to 10 percent as the market (hopefully) rallies. Why $1 million face value? That is the face value at which you can be sure of getting the best dealing price, since it is the minimum trading unit in the massive interdealer bond community. While there is no reason not to trade lesser amounts, and I would not discourage it, you may pay more per transaction since your IA's transfer price from the bond trading desk may be higher or lower depending on whether you are buying or selling. It also becomes of paramount importance to find the firm (and the IA) that will give you the best service; you cannot afford to be poorly serviced with bad pricing techniques. In fact, you may bargain for a certain commission rate per transaction, but even then, you will never really know what the transfer price is.

Charting the Bond Market

For those determined to trade the bond market aggressively or for those merely looking for information, charting the bond market is a must. Where do you find prices? Which bonds to chart? Your IA's firm may be able to provide you with charts, but they will not likely be what you want. You can build your own charts using pen and paper (squared works best), or (for those with a PC) simple spreadsheets can be built that take some of the drudgery away. First, where to get the prices? Assuming we are charting the Canadian bond market, the *Financial Post* and the *Globe and Mail* both produce bond quotations that represent the closing price levels from the day before, typically at 4:00 p.m. Since the bond market never really stops trading, participants have to pick a moment every day to declare a closing price. Which bonds do you chart? To speculate in bonds means you should trade the most active and liquid issues. In so doing, you will have a tight bid-ask spread and the assurance that there *will* be a bid and an ask. Therefore, you will be trading and charting the benchmark Government of Canada bonds, the key trading issues in the market at different maturities.

Today, the benchmark maturities are two, three, five, seven, ten, and thirty years. This is true in most global bond markets (although only Canada and the United States have thirty-year benchmark issues). What sets these issues apart from others is the amount of bonds outstanding. Wherever possible, the Bank of Canada will reopen a benchmark issue to provide market participants with increased liquidity at a key maturity. Normally, the bond will have what is called a "current coupon," one that is close to the prevailing interest rate at that maturity. What happens in the real world is that first, time passes — the former ten-year benchmark is now only eight years, for example, and a new ten-year has to be created — and second, bond prices rise or fall, putting the benchmark price at a large premium or discount. In this case, the central bank may wish to issue a more current coupon.

The *Financial Post* identifies the benchmark issues; therefore, you do not have to bother your IA. I would recommend that you chart the two-, five-, ten-, and thirty-year issues. For purposes of this chapter, we will use the Canada 5.75 percent maturing June 1, 2029, as our chosen benchmark to chart. Even though it is less than thirty years, it is the most actively traded long-term Canada bond. Also, as I mentioned in the chapter on products, it is in your best interest to begin charting the U.S. ten-year benchmark. Also, you might want to chart the Canadian ten-year.

Since we are intending to speculate, we should be charting the price of the bond, not the yield. You may wish to chart yields also, but what you will have will merely be the inverse of the price chart. Remember the dinosaur?

Moving Averages

Most serious chartists employ a series of moving averages and momentum to forecast bond prices. There are short-term trading charts, and medium- to long-term as well. I recommend you use the following moving average periods: ten days, thirty days, and two hundred days. For a momentum oscillator, use ten-day minus thirty-day moving averages. In moving average terms, you have a buy signal when the spot price is higher than the ten-day and thirty-day moving averages, all three lines are moving up, and the momentum oscillator is moving up and is above zero.

These are all commonly used tools for charting anything, stocks, bonds, gold, etc. If your IA cannot provide you with any price history to begin with, you can get back copies of the newspaper; this is better than starting from scratch since it will be a while before your charts will be complete — and think of all those money-making opportunities you might miss!

What is a moving average? It is an average of a given series of numbers that changes each day as new data is added and old data drops off. Consider the ten daily closes for the Government of Canada 5.75 percent due June 1, 2029:

18-Jul-05	120.412
19-Jul-05	120.870
20-Jul-05	120.800
21-Jul-05	120.150
22-Jul-05	121.170
25-Jul-05	121.400
26-Jul-05	121.080
27-Jul-05	120.910
28-Jul-05	121.690
29-Jul-05	121.600

Now, adding up these ten prices and dividing by ten, you end up with a ten-day average of $121.008. When we add another day, say August 1, the price is now $121.485; the moving average will change as we drop the $120.412 price and add the $121.48 price. The ten-day average is now $121.116, and so on. Since this changes each day, it is called a "moving average." Averaging smooths out day-to-day fluctuations to produce a graph of the price movement. Obviously, the longer the series the less impact a daily price change has. Let us look at our first chart, which tracks the daily price along with the ten-day and thirty-day moving averages.

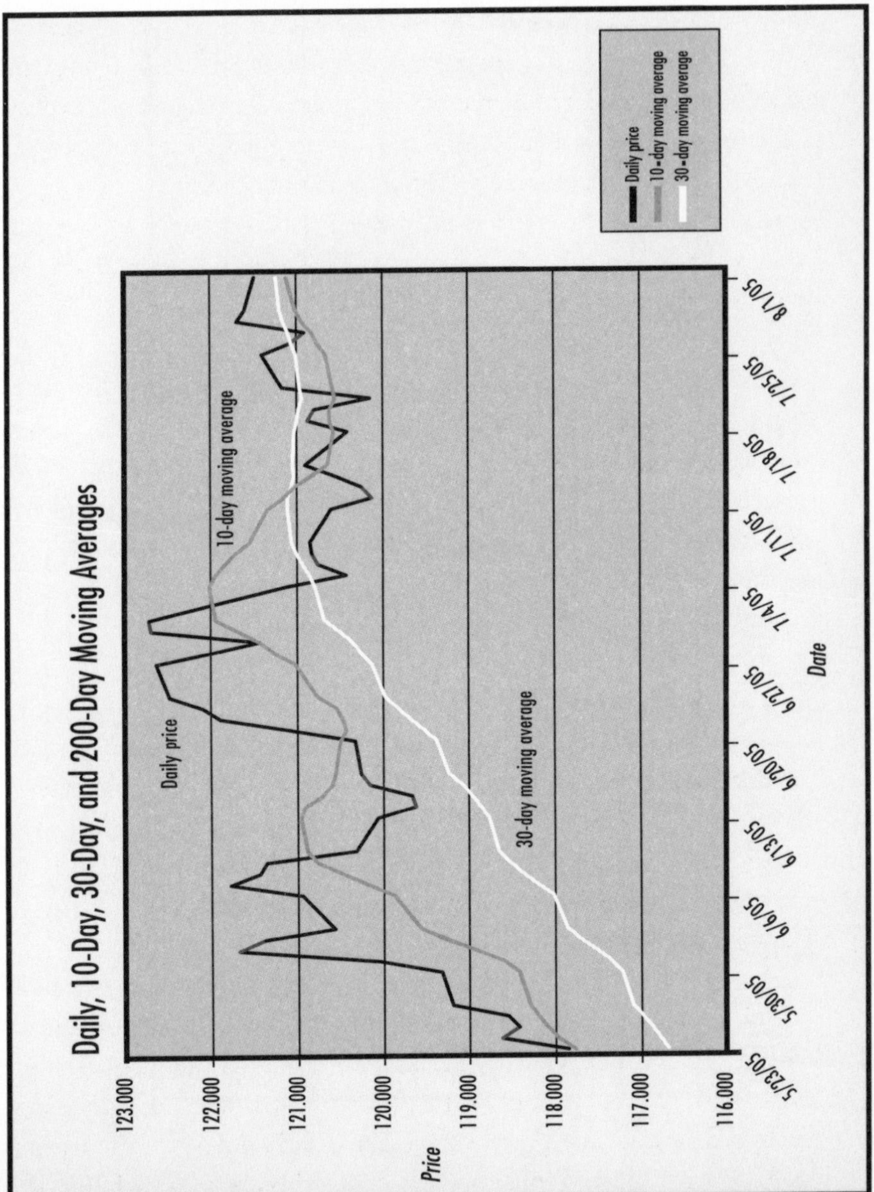

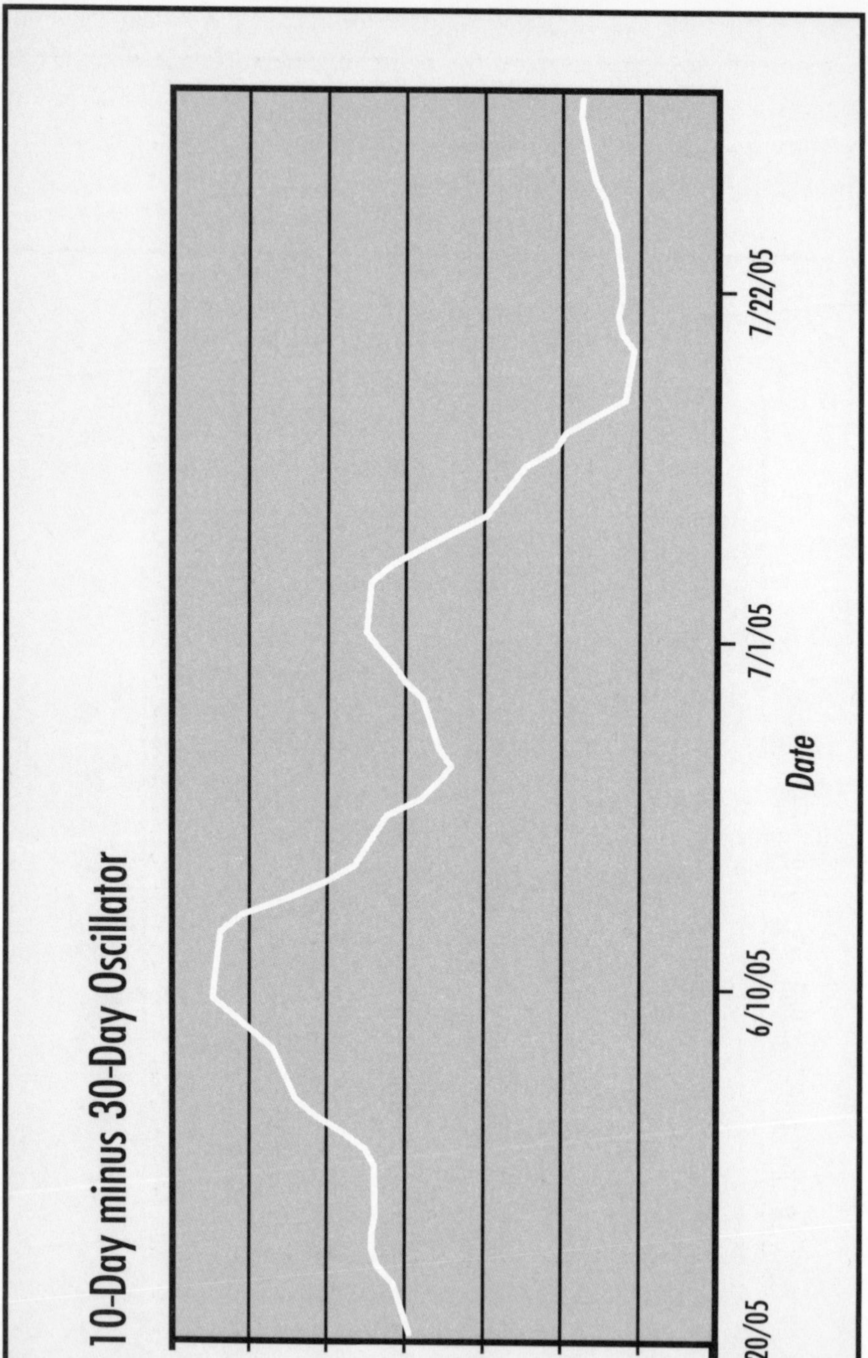
10-Day minus 30-Day Oscillator
2.5
2
1.5
1
0.5
0
-0.5
-1
5/20/05
6/10/05
7/1/05
7/22/05
Date

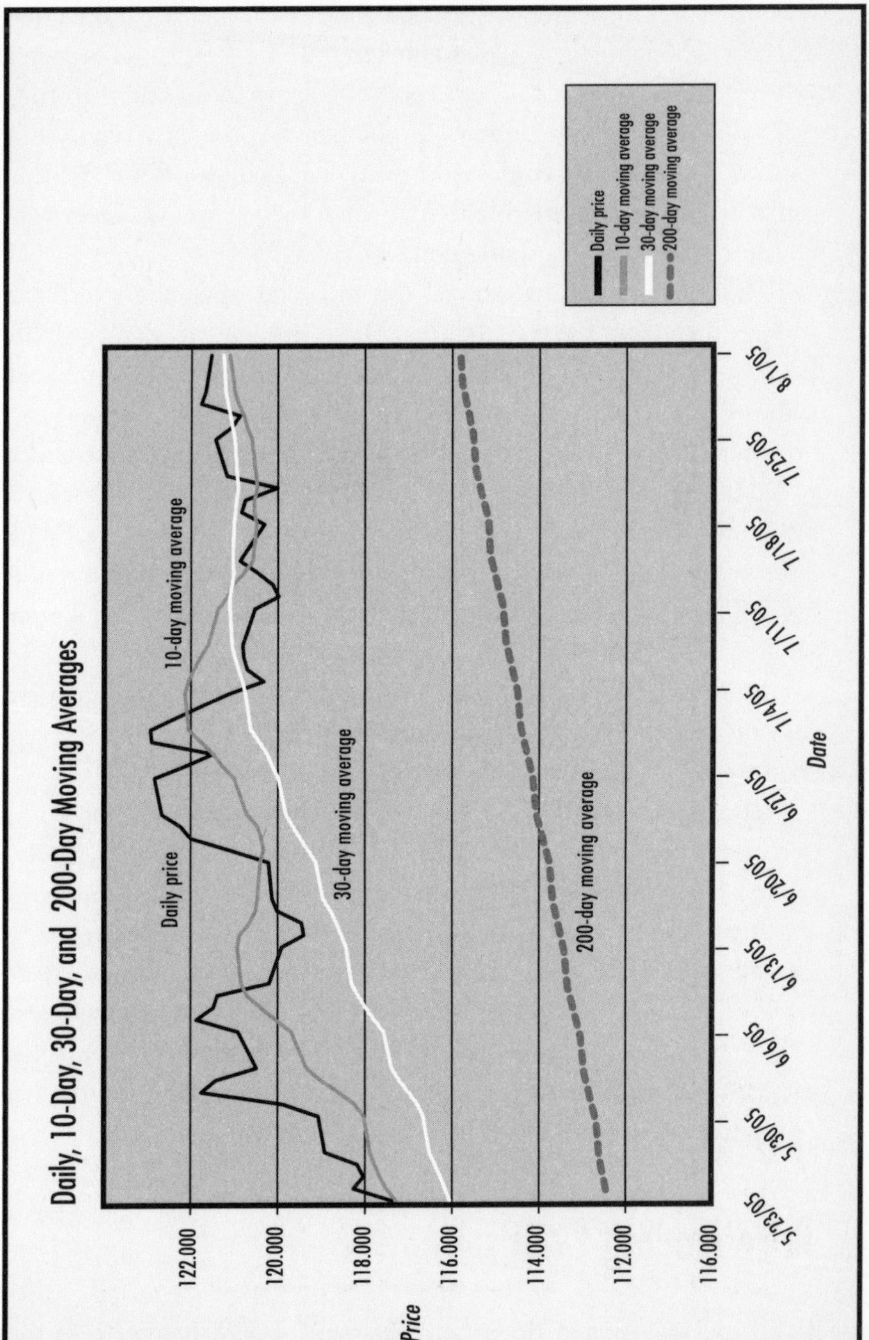
Daily, 10-Day, 30-Day, and 200-Day Moving Averages
Daily price
10-day moving average
30-day moving average
200-day moving average
Price
122.000
120.000
118.000
116.000
114.000
112.000
116.000
Date
5/23/05
5/30/05
6/6/05
6/13/05
6/20/05
6/27/05
7/4/05
7/11/05
7/18/05
7/25/05
8/1/05
Daily price
10-day moving average
30-day moving average
200-day moving average

What we see is the two averages moving in an up trend, but at different speeds. Classic moving average theory indicates that if the price and the two moving averages are moving in one direction, the trend will continue until the daily price starts to move lower and the other two averages eventually follow. As you can see, the gap widens and narrows between the ten-day and thirty-day averages. We chart this gap as an oscillator to be able to spot when the market becomes overbought or oversold on a short-term basis.

Thus, a speculator would sell (or go short) when the trend was strongly higher but the oscillator had hit an extreme rate of change. In the above example, the oscillator was at a very high level and, combined with the moving average chart, this represented a selling opportunity — or, to put it another way, a bad time to buy. A more conservative trader would wait for the moving averages to reverse and for the oscillator to move into negative territory. This chart is for short-term trading. Some cyclical perspective is important, since short-term moves against the cyclical trend may not last long. Therefore, we will now add the longer series, which smooths the data even more.

Despite the short-term selling opportunity, the two-hundred-day moving average is well below current prices, indicating that the long-term trend is still toward higher prices.

Clearly, charting is not a panacea for bond speculators, but it is a very useful tool for identifying opportunities and timing one's investments. Anyone intending to speculate in bonds should also arm themselves with a few other weapons. I would add that maintaining price charts such as these can be of considerable help when making an investment decision. If the market was severely overbought, or if a technical sell signal occurred, then you would wait until a better buying opportunity materialized. Conversely, a market that was oversold or for which a buy signal was in place would cause you to make your investment.

Price Moving Events

Bond speculators and investors in general should be aware of the constant parade of economic data as well as the issuance of new bonds, otherwise they could be sideswiped. The American and Canadian authorities release a calendar of forthcoming releases, the most important of which for the bond market are the inflation data, the employment market, and the GDP numbers. At different points in the economic cycle, different news may carry more weight. The American calendar is found in Barrons, while the Canadian one is in the weekend *Financial Post*. Your own IA or discount broker will be able to provide such a calendar along with consensus forecasts for the various releases. In any event, large price movements, sometimes irrational, follow the release of key data, providing the nimble trader with opportunity.

Auctions/New Issues

A feature of the bond market is the constant supply of new issues, as past debt matures and must be rolled over and as the deficit must be funded. Both the American and Canadian federal governments issue bonds via an auction method whereby a group of pre-authorized investment dealers bid for the issues and redistribute them to their client base. The auction schedule is known in advance in both countries. What is important to know for the would-be speculator is that the auction participants are not paid a commission for their role in the auction. What they must do to stay in business is sell the bonds at a slightly higher price than they paid for them. Therefore, there is little incentive to bid up the bond market aggressively before an auction, since that would increase the odds of being stuck with overpriced merchandise. Investment dealers do have an opportunity to pre-sell an auction issue in the "when-issued" (WI) market. As soon as the details of an auction are released, when-issued trading commences. This allows the participants to try and build a book for the auction by pre-selling it, and thus building up a short position with which to bid. This WI period provides opportunities for the nimble, as the auctioned issue may be offered cheaply.

In any event, large new supply can derail a bond market rally. Provincial borrowers do not release their borrowing calendar in advance and can cause some serious disruption to the market with large, surprise issues.

There are other tools you should arm yourself with.

The Bank of Canada weekly statement is chock full of key numbers, averages, and charts. Phone the Bank of Canada nearest you to get on the list or draw it into your PC. Its website is full of all kinds of useful information.

Without a doubt, the best buy in the Canadian financial marketplace is the *Bank of Canada Quarterly Review*, available for the incredibly low annual price of $25. It is a compendium of data, including timely articles, series of economic, financial and market tables and charts. It is a fabulous reference source.

My website provides updated charts, forthcoming economic and market moving events, and overview commentary.

If you conclude that using technical analysis can at least help save you money or add yield, then it is of value.

CONCLUSION

I have made my case in this book that careful selection of individual fixed-income products is in your best interest, as you can tailor your fixed-income investment portfolio to suit your individual needs. I have attempted to arm you with the appropriate tools and information.

The laddered approach is a simple enough concept, but in practice it is a very disciplined and effective approach to investing. Zero coupon bonds, combined with the laddered approach, are important investments for retirement planning purposes. Using this approach leads to what I call the sleep-at-night portfolio, where you will have assembled investments that are most beneficial to you.

As I mentioned in the introduction, when asked how the bond market functions, I blurted out that it was all about relationships. The more I pondered this remark, the more I realized that this was an essential truth. Your relationship with your investment advisor is all-important to your financial well-being, and so I dedicated a chapter in this book discussing how to choose the right IA. Also, you have learned that most fixed-income products trade in relation to something else. A certain bond may be matrix priced to a specific benchmark, to a yield curve, to the bank rate, or to the prime lending rate.

In addition, from my perspective, after trading over a trillion dollars of fixed-income securities with nary a hitch, my relationships with my traders, my counterparties (the other investment dealers with whom I transact business), my clients (all the IAs and smaller financial organizations that I service), and the rest of my own firm are very important. I owe most of my success to the people who have worked with me and made me look good. These people, many of whom are smarter than I am, have similar strengths. They are all intelligent, hard-working individuals of the highest integrity and possess the most valuable of all traits for my business: tremendous interpersonal skills. They all know how to offer pleasant but excellent service to IAs, they have represented me in the street exceptionally well, and they have maintained strong corporate relationships.

Either one has it or one does not. As any manager will say, the hiring process is vitally important, and despite our best efforts, we make bad hires or exercise bad judgment. In my case, my success ratio is very high. Over the years, a large number of people have approached me to be a bond trader, lured mostly by the glamour and the money.

I have been approached at office parties, in bars, and by phone and e-mail. Some applicants were aggressive, some attempted to pull strings, while others just sent in resumes and then harassed me. It was thus a challenge to separate the glamour seekers from the genuine candidates. The extent that I succeeded is partly owed to the road-less-travelled approach I followed in the investment business.

To help weed out the wannabes, I concocted a simple test to see how they would react to a tiny bit of pressure. I had read the book *Hard Drive* by Bill Gates, in which he described the hiring process that Microsoft used when interviewing. Besides the formal interview process, Microsoft threw in a series of up to twenty random questions to see how the applicants would perform on the spot. This seemed like a good idea to me, so I thought up a couple of what I thought were innocent questions appropriate to my business. What followed was a most educational experience. I would be at a bar or a party and an individual would screw up the courage (or perhaps swallow some liquid courage!) and approach me. Typically, I would know the individual already, but sometimes he or she knew about me but had never met me.

What followed had a predictable outcome. The individuals would tell me why they would make good traders or who they knew. At some point, I would ask how good their math was, and the answer was normally "excellent" or "very good." Then I would quietly ask them to answer a simple question: "What is 1/8 of 1 percent of $100,000?" This was the first of two questions, as this one was so easy I had a backup question. Well, what happened next bordered on the unbelievable! They panicked, froze, guessed, refused to answer, told me it was a stupid question, blurted out different answers, or just stomped off. Very few (maybe 2 percent) actually stopped, thought on their feet, and arrived at the answer. People have accused me of employing an inappropriate question, as my generation learned math without calculators. That may be true, but I was looking for people who could stay cool under pressure and use logic. What I was not looking for were robots! The thought process should go something like this:

10 percent of $100,000 = $10,000 so 1 percent would therefore be $1,000. One-eighth of that is $125.

Almost no one had .125 anywhere in the answer (.125, of course, is 1/8 in decimal form!) Needless to say, those who stayed cool and used logic usually got the job! However, that was only after answering the second question, which was, "What is 1/4 of 1 percent of $250,000?" These questions and answers were germane to my business, as the results were typical of the small trading profits (or losses) I would frequently make.

There was no typical hire; none of my hires were MBAs or math grads. I have hired chemistry majors, philosophy majors, some who had not finished university, and some who only had secondary school education. I was visited once by the Dean of Business from the University of Toronto, who toured Bay Street asking various managers what they were looking for. I replied that the two most important factors were that a candidate must display excellent interpersonal skills and also be literate! A trading department deals with a multitude of personalities. My traders had to represent me professionally with the street, deal comfortably with all levels of the company, and, most importantly, deal effectively with every kind of human behaviour imaginable in the large number of IAs that we serviced.

Also important were literacy and presentation skills. Raw ability just was not good enough. I often sent my traders to presentation skills development or similar courses to augment their already wonderful traits.

So relationships are important, and so is integrity.

The investment business has not been without its share of scandals, promotions, hype, and bad IAs. There are only two paths to follow, and I have chosen the high road. By this I mean always conducting my business with honesty and integrity, and transmitting these values to everyone with whom I have had the pleasure of working.

We have only a few tools to work with: computers, the phone, and what is between our ears. What people remember is how they are treated. Thus, one's name is crucial, and I am very proud of the name I have established. As someone who has traded trillions of dollars of fixed-income securities over a span of some thirty-five years on an over-the counter basis, I can say that I have never had any serious disputes with counterparties. Your word is your bond in this business; once it is given, you are done!

I have had to let traders go who hid transactions from me or who did not represent me professionally. In this business, you are only as good as your weakest link. I have built four trading departments from scratch, each of them successful and each of them full of bright people with a high level of integrity and strong interpersonal skills.

I am pleased to say that, in a male-dominated business, I have always had an above-average ratio of female traders, and this was not lip service, as they are very smart with tremendous interpersonal skills. All of those young women and men who worked for me made me look good and I sincerely hope that I have taught them something and that I helped make them into better people.

In the fixed income business, billions of dollars of fixed-income securities trade on the basis of a verbal handshake. Admittedly, all our conversations are now taped, but there are almost never any serious trade disputes, as any misunderstandings or differences of opinion are resolved right away. Interestingly, the most serious debates have involved trades between my desk and retail IAs. Sometimes IAs will dispute a trade or a price, convinced that we have somehow done them wrong. As soon as we announce we are going to listen to the tapes, 99 percent of these problems go away! Also, when we review the production records of the IAs in question, they are normally in the bottom 20 percent of commissions, spending too much time on disputes and not enough with their clients. Sometimes I will review the complaint and decide that an IA had a point; however, most of the time, the IA doesn't pass the improved price on to the clients but pockets the difference.

I hope that you have learned something from reading this book and that you now feel more empowered to enhance your returns. I wrote it in your best interest.

Appendix A

List of Websites

www.bankofcanada.ca **(Excellent)**
www.bloomberg.com
www.bondcan.com
www.bondsonline.com
www.bondtalk.com **(Excellent)**
www.canada.com
www.dbrs.com
www.fool.com
www.globeinvestor.com
www.ida.ca
www.independentfinancial.on.ca
www.investinginbonds.com **(Good Q and A, links to other sites)**
www.investopedia.com
www.investorlearning.ca
www.inyourbestinterest.ca
www.iunits.com
www.newyorkfed.org
www.osc.ca
www.smartmoney.com
www.standardandpoors.com
www.stockhouse.ca

Appendix B

Present Value Table

2.00%	2.50%	3.00%	3.50%	4.00%	4.50%	5.00%	5.50%	6.00%
0.980392	0.975610	0.970874	0.966184	0.961538	0.956938	0.952381	0.947867	0.943396
0.961169	0.951814	0.942596	0.933511	0.924556	0.915730	0.907029	0.898452	0.889996
0.942322	0.928599	0.915142	0.901943	0.888996	0.876297	0.863838	0.851614	0.839619
0.923845	0.905951	0.888487	0.871442	0.854804	0.838561	0.822702	0.807217	0.792094
0.905731	0.883854	0.862609	0.841973	0.821927	0.802451	0.783526	0.765134	0.747258
0.887971	0.862297	0.837484	0.813501	0.790315	0.767896	0.746215	0.725246	0.704961
0.870560	0.841265	0.813092	0.785991	0.759918	0.734828	0.710681	0.687437	0.665057
0.853490	0.820747	0.789409	0.759412	0.730690	0.703185	0.676839	0.651599	0.627412
0.836755	0.800728	0.766417	0.733731	0.702587	0.672904	0.644609	0.617629	0.591898
0.820348	0.781198	0.744094	0.708919	0.675564	0.643928	0.613913	0.585431	0.558395
0.804263	0.762145	0.722421	0.684946	0.649581	0.616199	0.584679	0.554911	0.526788
0.788493	0.743556	0.701380	0.661783	0.624597	0.589664	0.556837	0.525982	0.496969
0.773033	0.725420	0.680951	0.639404	0.600574	0.564272	0.530321	0.498561	0.468839
0.757875	0.707727	0.661118	0.617782	0.577475	0.539973	0.505068	0.472569	0.442301
0.743015	0.690466	0.641862	0.596891	0.555265	0.516720	0.481017	0.447933	0.417265
0.728446	0.673625	0.623167	0.576706	0.533908	0.494469	0.458112	0.424581	0.393646
0.714163	0.657195	0.605016	0.557204	0.513373	0.473176	0.436297	0.402447	0.371364
0.700159	0.641166	0.587395	0.538361	0.493628	0.452800	0.415521	0.381466	0.350344
0.686431	0.625528	0.570286	0.520156	0.474642	0.433302	0.395734	0.361579	0.330513
0.672971	0.610271	0.553676	0.502566	0.456387	0.414643	0.376889	0.342729	0.311805
0.659776	0.595386	0.537549	0.485571	0.438834	0.396787	0.358942	0.324862	0.294155
0.646839	0.580865	0.521893	0.469151	0.421955	0.379701	0.341850	0.307926	0.277505
0.634156	0.566697	0.506692	0.453286	0.405726	0.363350	0.325571	0.291873	0.261797
0.621721	0.552875	0.491934	0.437957	0.390121	0.347703	0.310068	0.276657	0.246979
0.609531	0.539391	0.477606	0.423147	0.375117	0.332731	0.295303	0.262234	0.232999
0.597579	0.526235	0.463695	0.408838	0.360689	0.318402	0.281241	0.248563	0.219810
0.585862	0.513400	0.450189	0.395012	0.346817	0.304691	0.267848	0.235605	0.207368
0.574375	0.500878	0.437077	0.381654	0.333477	0.291571	0.255094	0.223322	0.195630
0.563112	0.488661	0.424346	0.368748	0.320651	0.279015	0.242946	0.211679	0.184557
0.552071	0.476743	0.411987	0.356278	0.308319	0.267000	0.231377	0.200644	0.174110

2.00%	2.50%	3.00%	3.50%	4.00%	4.50%	5.00%	5.50%	6.00%
0.541246	0.465115	0.399987	0.344230	0.296460	0.255502	0.220359	0.190184	0.164255
0.530633	0.453771	0.388337	0.332590	0.285058	0.244500	0.209866	0.180269	0.154957
0.520229	0.442703	0.377026	0.321343	0.274094	0.233971	0.199873	0.170871	0.146186
0.510028	0.431905	0.366045	0.310476	0.263552	0.223896	0.190355	0.161963	0.137912
0.500028	0.421371	0.355383	0.299977	0.253415	0.214254	0.181290	0.153520	0.130105
0.490223	0.411094	0.345032	0.289833	0.243669	0.205028	0.172657	0.145516	0.122741
0.480611	0.401067	0.334983	0.280032	0.234297	0.196199	0.164436	0.137930	0.115793
0.471187	0.391285	0.325226	0.270562	0.225285	0.187750	0.156605	0.130739	0.109239
0.461948	0.381741	0.315754	0.261413	0.216621	0.179665	0.149148	0.123924	0.103056
0.452890	0.372431	0.306557	0.252572	0.208289	0.171929	0.142046	0.117463	0.097222
0.444010	0.363347	0.297628	0.244031	0.200278	0.164525	0.135282	0.111339	0.091719
0.435304	0.354485	0.288959	0.235779	0.192575	0.157440	0.128840	0.105535	0.086527
0.426769	0.345839	0.280543	0.227806	0.185168	0.150661	0.122704	0.100033	0.081630
0.418401	0.337404	0.272372	0.220102	0.178046	0.144173	0.116861	0.094818	0.077009
0.410197	0.329174	0.264439	0.212659	0.171198	0.137964	0.111297	0.089875	0.072650
0.402154	0.321146	0.256737	0.205468	0.164614	0.132023	0.105997	0.085190	0.068538
0.394268	0.313313	0.249259	0.198520	0.158283	0.126338	0.100949	0.080748	0.064658
0.386538	0.305671	0.241999	0.191806	0.152195	0.120898	0.096142	0.076539	0.060998
0.378958	0.298216	0.234950	0.185320	0.146341	0.115692	0.091564	0.072549	0.057546
0.371528	0.290942	0.228107	0.179053	0.140713	0.110710	0.087204	0.068767	0.054288
0.364243	0.283846	0.221463	0.172998	0.135301	0.105942	0.083051	0.065182	0.051215
0.357101	0.276923	0.215013	0.167148	0.130097	0.101380	0.079096	0.061783	0.048316
0.350099	0.270169	0.208750	0.161496	0.125093	0.097014	0.075330	0.058563	0.045582
0.343234	0.263579	0.202670	0.156035	0.120282	0.092837	0.071743	0.055509	0.043001
0.336504	0.257151	0.196767	0.150758	0.115656	0.088839	0.068326	0.052616	0.040567
0.329906	0.250879	0.191036	0.145660	0.111207	0.085013	0.065073	0.049873	0.038271
0.323437	0.244760	0.185472	0.140734	0.106930	0.081353	0.061974	0.047273	0.036105
0.317095	0.238790	0.180070	0.135975	0.102817	0.077849	0.059023	0.044808	0.034061
0.310878	0.232966	0.174825	0.131377	0.098863	0.074497	0.056212	0.042472	0.032133
0.304782	0.227284	0.169733	0.126934	0.095060	0.071289	0.053536	0.040258	0.030314

GLOSSARY

Accretion – (*See* Amortization)

Accrued interest – Interest that adds up daily between interest payment dates. It is paid to investors on interest payment dates or on the settlement date if investors sell between interest payment dates.

Amortization – From the Latin *a mort*, "to death." This refers to the process where, as time passes, your fixed-income investment moves inexorably to its face or maturing value.

Ask – The price at which a bond trader is willing to sell a certain fixed-income instrument. *Offer* is sometimes used to mean the same thing but can lead to confusion, because if you ask someone to make you an offer, they might think you want a bid. Stick to ask.

Balloon – The maturing principal of a bond issue.

Bank of Canada – Canada's central bank. Its responsibilities focus on the goals of low and stable inflation, a safe and secure currency, financial stability, and the efficient management of government funds and public debt.

Bank rate – The minimum interest rate at which the Bank of Canada extends short-term loans.

Basis point – How everything gets measured (e.g., so many basis points over Canadas). A basis point is one one-hundredth of 1 percent. Thus, if the bank rate falls 25 basis points, it is the same as 0.25 (or 1/4) of 1 percent.

Bellwether – Essentially the same as benchmark, although its use refers to those issues media and market commentators refer to when describing the bond market's direction. The bellwether is a proxy for the market itself. Because of an active crowd of speculators, an issue may remain a bellwether while being replaced as a benchmark. For many years the Canada 8 percent bond due June 1, 2023, was the bellwether for the long-term market, even when it rose to $135 when interest rates fell. The major dealers used it for speculative purposes, to hedge inventories, and to price other new issues and their own long-term bond inventories. Market commentators pointed to this bond to give an idea of how the market was behaving. Speculators, both individual and institutional, continued to play this issue even after the market had gone up 20 points.

Benchmark – Bonds by which others are valued. The Bank of Canada (and some provinces) issue and reissue bonds at strategic maturity points (typically two, three, five, ten, and thirty years). These bonds become sizeable enough that they trade freely with tight bid-ask spreads. When issuers bring new bonds to market, the presence of these issues makes pricing easier since accurate market yields are readily available as references. Retail investors are wise to stick to benchmark issues, as retail desks are more likely to maintain inventory and have lower transfer prices for them since the turnover is higher. Benchmarks are eventually replaced by new ones, since the passage of time leaves gaps at the key maturities (e.g., a five-year bond becomes a four-year bond one year later). Or interest rates may change significantly, leaving the benchmark issue with too high or too low a coupon for practical use.

Bid – What a bond trader is willing to pay for a certain bond.

Bond – (*See also* Debentures) A security issued by a government or corporation paying fixed or floating interest payments. There is a *bond* between borrower and lender. It is also used in a broader sense to describe the bond market.

Bond trader – An individual who makes markets in bonds.

Bonus – What bond traders are paid for skilful trading.

Book – The number of clients o an IA and the amount of assets in total that the clients have. Ask about an IA's book: how many clients, size of assets, turnover, number of sales assistants, composition, etc.

Book-based – The electronic record of who owns what. The days of physical securities (actual pieces of paper) are almost totally over.

Broker – Terms such as *investment advisors*, *financial advisors*, *investment executives*, and *financial planners* have been introduced to give a warm and fuzzy feeling to your investment-making decisions.

Callable – With a call feature, the borrower may prematurely pay off the loan. As a lender, you do not want this to happen. If you call the peak in interest rates accurately, buying long-term bonds at attractive yields for twenty years, the last thing you want is to get your money back in ten years should rates fall, forcing you to reinvest at the then prevailing lower yields. Only the borrower may call the issue. Today, most bond issues are non-callable for financial advantage. Past callable issues still trade and are often quoted in the weekend newspapers. The quoted yield is much higher than other bonds but reflects the fact that they may be called soon. The bigger the gap between the coupon rate on a callable bond and existing market rates, the greater the certainty that the issue will be called and refinanced.

Call loan – How investment dealers finance themselves. Also called overnight money. Dealers post their inventory as collateral. This rate is every bit as important as the bank rate — ask your IA what the overnight rate is sometime! The Bank of Canada influences money market rates by altering the amount of cash in the system.

Cold call – A phone call, not solicited by the party being phoned, from an IA; typically, it is a new IA or a junior or someone whose business has fallen. Sales managers give quotas to such IAs and so they interrupt people at work or at home in order to impress upon them that they should move their entire investment portfolio immediately. Anyone who has to make cold calls is not successful. If it suits you, ask them a few skill-testing questions or for some performance stats.

Compound interest – Interest earned by reinvesting interest payments; or interest on interest.

Convertible bonds – Issued with a coupon rate and a maturity date like most bonds, but also carrying a feature which gives investors the right to convert their debt to equity on specific terms.

Convexity – The second derivative of duration.

Credit – From the Latin *credere*, "to believe." When you invest in a fixed-income security, you believe that the borrower will pay you back.

Credit rating – The likelihood that a borrower will pay you back. Credit rating agencies assess the financial strength of issuers. The most well known are Standard and Poors, Moody's, and Dominion Bond Rating Service.

Debenture – A "bond" issued with no specific collateral to back it. Strictly speaking, government bonds are actually debentures.

Defeasance – Offsetting a future liability with an asset of similar maturity and amount. Strips are commonly used to defease a future debt as they can be invested to a precise future value.

Discount rate – A symbolic rate. Nominally, a rate at which a central bank will advance funds to approved borrowers. It is an instrument of monetary policy; a change in the Discount rate is a signal to the market place that the central bank wants market rates to move in the direction signaled. As well, in the event of emergencies, where a credit crunch is taking place, loans will actually take place at the discount window. Small "d" discount refers to a rate applied to a future sum to arrive at a present value. It also refers to bonds trading at less than their face value.

Duration – The average life of your fixed-income investment. A ten-year bond is not a ten-year bond. All those pesky interest payments shorten the average term. The bigger the interest payments, the shorter the duration. For a zero coupon bond, maturity and duration are the same since there are no cash flows to worry about. Duration is used by bond cognoscenti as a way of measuring risk.

Face value – The stated nominal value of your fixed-income investment. For example, you invest $98,000 in a bond that matures to $100,000. The $100,000 is the face value of the bond. The market price may go above or below that value, but that is what will be returned to you.

Fixed – A rate of interest paid by a borrower on a bond that stays constant.

Flat – A yield curve where yields are the same at all maturities. Can also mean that a bond is trading with no accrued interest, either because the settlement date coincides with the coupon payment date or else because the issuer is not able to make interest payments.

Floating – A rate of interest that is adjusted at specific intervals using a specific formula. For example, every three months at three month treasury bills plus 25 basis points.

GICs – Also pronounced "geeks." These are securities issued by banks so that they can lend your money out at a higher rate.

Hedge – What bond traders do to protect their inventories from market fluctuation. Typically, it involves selling short benchmark issues against long positions.

IDA – Investment Dealers Association. A self-regulatory body for all the investment dealer members.

IDB – Interdealer broker. An intermediary that facilitates trade between investment dealers by posting anonymous bids and offerings.

Institutions – Large financial organizations, namely life insurance, pension funds, mutual funds, governments, and banks, make up the bulk of bond market activity. They represent the individual investor since they are trading other people's money — your pension, mutual fund units, bank deposits, etc.

Interest –Money paid to investors by borrowers for lending them money. Similar to a landlord/tenant relationship. Interest payments are thus analogous to rent payments.

Inventory – To facilitate the retail and institutional customers, investment dealers maintain inventory of "shelf products," financed with their own capital and which are offered at hopefully competitive prices.

Investment dealers – Organizations that provide a wide range of services to both issuers of securities and those who invest in them. They provide market making ability in money and bond markets, underwriting capability, and brokerage services, among others.

Jobbers – Approved money market dealers who must bid for each week's treasury bill auction. They are Bank of Montreal, CIBC, Deutsche Bank Securities, Laurentian Bank, Merrill Lynch Canada, National Bank Financial, RBC Dominion Securities, Scotia Capital, and Toronto Dominion Bank.

Junk bonds – Bonds issued by companies whose credit ratings have fallen below levels considered safe for investors. Their relative and absolute high yields reflect how risky they are.

Leverage – What you use to get better prices by threatening to take your business elsewhere. Refers to buying bonds on margin. Long Canadas are marginable at 4 percent for investment dealers and typically 10 percent for individuals. That represents considerable leverage.

Liquidity –The relative ease by which investors may buy or sell bonds.

Long position – A bond position owned in inventory by an investment dealer.

Management fees – What you pay a mutual fund manager to gamble with your money. Also known as management expense ratios, or MERs.

Margin – Money loaned to you by an FI to finance a leveraged position.

Markup – The amount that IAs add to the transfer price from their bond desk in order to get paid.

Matrix – Establishing a price for a bond by linking it to a more actively traded issue in order to provide a quotation.

Maturity – The point in time at which your fixed-income investment comes to an end and your principal or face value is returned to you.

Monetary policy – Carried out by the Bank of Canada, it is a policy that either stimulates or restricts money supply growth by either lowering or raising interest rates or by expanding or contracting bank reserves.

Money market – Fixed-income securities issued with a term to maturity of one year or less. It is also applied to those bonds issued with a maturity date longer than one year but whose maturities have now reached less than one year owing to the passage of time.

Mutual funds – Entities that take your money and mingle it with a whole lot of other people's money and pay themselves handsomely in the process.

Offer – (*See also* Ask) Opposite of a bid. It is the price at which a trader is willing to sell a bond.

Off the run – A bond issue that is not a benchmark issue. It may have a very high or low coupon; it may be a small, illiquid issue; its ownership may be concentrated in few hands; or it may have a feature that makes it unattractive to trade — the bid-ask spread will be wider for such an issue, as dealers either do not wish to hold them in inventory or find it difficult to sell them quickly. This sometimes works in the favour of the client, but not often, as the transfer price is typically higher than it would be if the issue was "on the run."

On the run – An actively traded bond whose coupon rate is close to current yield levels so that its price is close to par.

Over the counter – Something that is not centralized. Unlike the equity market, which has a recognizable physical location to trade stocks, the bond market is decentralized, with no one meeting place; transactions occur verbally or electronically between market participants. Bonds trade on a principal basis. Unlike equities, where buyers and sellers meet to trade a stock and charge each client a commission, bonds trade on a net basis — dealers maintain inventories of fixed-income products, financing them with their own capital and attempting to sell them at slightly higher prices than they paid. At the retail level, it is similar to a store. The dealers maintain "shelf product," marking up from wholesale to compensate for risk, cost of capital, etc. They must maintain competitive pricing since they are selling the same line of goods as their principal competitors.

Par – A price of $100. Bonds mature at par, or 100 percent of their face value.

Performance – What your investments return.

Present value –What an amount of money due in the future is worth today after applying a discount rate.

Primary dealers – Those investment dealers chosen by the Bank of Canada to bid for new issues and make orderly secondary markets for Government of Canada issues. At present there are eleven primary dealers: BMO Nesbitt Burns, Casgrain and Co., CIBC World Markets, Deutsche Bank Securities, Merrill Lynch Canada, J.P. Morgan Securities Canada, Laurentian Bank Securities, National Bank Financial, RBC Dominion Securities, Scotia Capital, and Toronto Dominion Bank.

Positive – Refers to a "normal" yield curve, one where the longer the term to maturity the higher the yield. Also known as upward-sloping.

Principal – What you lend. It is returned to you at maturity date.

Principle – What you hope your IA has lots of.

Reconstitution – The reverse of stripping: putting a bond back together again.

Redeemable – Similar to callable bonds but with one huge difference: normally issued by corporations, a redeemable bond may not be called by the issuer for financial advantage. In other words, the issue may not be redone at a lower coupon rate. Rather, should a company have surplus cash or in the event of a corporate development (e.g. a takeover), the bond issue may be retired prematurely.

Reinvestment risk – There are two basic risks. First, the yield to maturity quoted on a bond may not be realized since all interest payments never get reinvested at the same rate. Second, having your entire portfolio mature at the same time is a financial version of Russian roulette. Rates may have fallen dramatically, leaving you much poorer.

Residuals – The principal portion left over after all the interest payments have been stripped away. (We do not call them principals, because that would be easy to understand!)

Registered Retirement Savings Plan (RRSP) – A plan that allows individuals to defer tax until retirement.

Semi-annual – For bonds, twice a year. Most bonds pay interest on a semi-annual basis. Do not be tricked into buying any biennial pay bonds!

Short-selling – Selling a security that one does not own. Typically used by investment dealers to hedge long positions, to accommodate client demands, or to speculate on falling bond prices.

Sinking fund – There are two types of sinking funds. The first is found on older corporate bonds: it is a feature that says that a company must redeem a certain percentage of an issue each year before maturity. This reduces the burden of paying an entire issue off at one date and also reduces the debt in proportion to the depreciation of the asset built or purchased with the proceeds. It also provides for liquidity, since the issuing company provides bids for the bonds; however, should interest rates fall, the company redeems the bonds at par or face value — not a welcome development for the lender since the bonds should trade at a premium! In the good old days when there was a thriving corporate bond market, institutional bond jockeys would play the "sinking fund game," corralling large blocks in an attempt to get the sinker to pay a higher price than justified by the credit. Steadily declining rates in the last twelve years have brought home to many the negative side of these features that may see their investment prematurely terminated. A second type of sinking fund is a general sinking fund. Normally issued by provinces, this feature indicates that the borrower must set aside a certain percentage of money every year but does not have to buy that specific one. This adds to liquidity and allows the issuer to invest in bonds (frequently stripped bonds) to allow for the orderly repayment of the bond issue at maturity.

Spread – The difference between the bid side and the offered side of a bond quotation. The shorter the bond and the higher the quality of the bond, the closer or "tighter" the bid-ask spread. Benchmark issues trade tighter than other bonds. Small corporate bond issues with little float may not even have a two-sided market. The spread thus incorporates a trader's feel for how quickly a bond may be sold.

Strips – Zero coupon bonds that pay no interest. Zeros, residuals, TIGRs, Sentinels, and Cougars, are all the same. They are excellent for retirement planning, as they trade at a discount from par or maturing value; the size of the discount will depend on the amount of time to maturity and the yield to maturity.

Stripping – Separating the components of a bond — interest payments and the principal — and selling them all as separate zero coupon securities.

Switches – Transactions or trades where one bond is exchanged or traded for another for any one of a number of reasons — to shorten term, extend term, pick up yield, improve quality, etc.

Transfer price – The price at which the bond-trading desk transfers a bond to an IA. In other words, the salesperson's cost. To make a living, the salesperson must add a commission to this cost. The client does not see this since bonds are quoted on a "net" or "all-in" basis. The transfer price will vary from one investment dealer to another and is a function of the philosophy and structure of that organization. The lower the transfer price, the lower the cost to the client. The corollary is that a broker facing a higher transfer price may have to reduce markup in order to remain competitive and thus face lower earnings.

Transparency – The ease of being able to view bond quotations and transactions. The Canadian bond market is more opaque than transparent.

Unit holder – One who owns units in a mutual fund.

Volatility – How much the price of a bond changes for a given movement in yield.

Yield – Current, to maturity. Basically, what an investment returns. Current yield of a bond is the coupon rate divided by the price. This is also known as "running yield." However, it is misleading, as bonds have a maturity date and the difference between the market price and the value at maturity must be factored into the yield.

Yield curve – A line drawn joining yields at different maturity dates.

Zero coupon bonds – (*See* Strips)